Faith and Race

One Church's Response

to the Civil Rights Movement

Faith and Race

One Church's Response to the Civil Rights Movement

Melynda Dovel Wilcox

© 2023 Melynda Dovel Wilcox

Westminster Presbyterian Church
2701 Cameron Mills Road
Alexandria, VA 22302

All rights reserved. No part of this book may be reproduced in any form, or by any electronic, mechanical, or other means, without permission in writing from the author.

First edition

Faith and Race: One Church's Response
to the Civil Rights Movement

Wilcox, Melynda Dovel, 1963– author
Cover and book design: Ellen Johnson Hamilton, granddaughter of Clifford R. Johnson
Cover: Photo by Charles Winburn for Westminster Presbyterian Church.

Photos and images are courtesy of Westminster Presbyterian Church unless otherwise noted.

Library of Congress Control Number:
2023907776

ISBN 978-0-9763725-4-7

Produced in Alexandria, Virginia
Manufactured in the United States of America

Yellow Dot Publishing
Alexandria, VA 22301
yellowdotpublishing.com

CONTENTS

Preface 7

Introduction 9

Part I: The Cliff Johnson Era 13

Filling the Pews 13

Speaking Freely and Frankly 15

Confronting Racism 17

Confessing His Own Prejudices 20

Venturing Policy Prescriptions 23

Foreseeing the Future 28

Part II: Connie Ring: Faith in Action in the Community 31

Early Interest in Public Service 31

Forming Key Alliances 33

At the Center of the City's Struggle Toward School Integration 34

Reaching Across Many Aisles 37

Part III: The Evolution of Westminster's Congregation 39

Presidential Visit 39

Nestled in a Segregated Neighborhood 42

Church Leaders and Members React and Respond 44

Community Collaborations 53

"Have I Made a Mistake?" 55

Pandemic, Racial Reckoning and Personal Tragedy 59

Conclusion 67

Acknowledgments 69

Appendix 71

Therefore Committee Report to the Westminster Presbyterian Church Session 71

Therefore Committee Members 72

Recommendations 73

Guiding Principles When Dealing with Social and Political Issues 74

Timeline 74

Origins of the Therefore Committee Project 75

Bibliography 77

About the Author 81

PREFACE

Following the murder of George Floyd on May 25, 2020, the Session of Westminster Presbyterian Church (Alexandria, Virginia) established the Therefore Project Committee to evaluate Westminster's past and present as a congregation concerning racial issues facing our country. Over the next eight months, the committee was formed, completed its work, and developed nine recommendations, which the Session adopted in full on June 23, 2021. One of the recommendations called for the church to write a history of Westminster relative to race. This manuscript fulfills that recommendation.

(The full report from the Therefore Committee to the Session is included in the Appendix. The Recommendations section of the report was adopted unanimously; the Guiding Principles section was approved by a vote of 16 to 12.)

In chronicling Westminster's history as it relates to the civil rights movement, this research project endeavors to present as honest an interpretation of these events as possible given the resources and information available. Some terms, such as "Negro" and "colored," that are offensive relative to the standards and sensibilities of 2023 are used here in specific quotations in order to reflect accurately the original source material. Some statements can be jarring and painful to read today, particularly given that they were spoken from the Westminster pulpit.

Stylistic decisions regarding terminology around race and ethnicity, such as capitalizing Black but not white, were made after consulting a careful review of academic research and current style guides undertaken by the Brookings Institution in 2020. Standards will no doubt continue to evolve as time passes, so the terms used here will inevitably appear dated to future readers.

Emphases shown in quoted material match those in the original sources. This manuscript originally appeared on the Westminster website as "Westminster and the Civil Rights Movement: Cliff, Connie and a Congregation" (www.wpc-alex.org).

"Dear God, please help us to recognize as Christians that every aspect of our nation's political life is our Christian concern, and that if our social order is to survive and improve, it is only as we as Christians dare to face the implication of its problems, and if this church is to be a true branch of the Church of our Lord Jesus Christ, dear God, it must be as we determine and make it so. And finally, heavenly Father, there's not any one of us bowing before Thee but who is aware that there are areas of our personal lives that deeply need to become matters of concern. Wilt Thou help us, O God, to have the courage and the commitment to make them so. This we pray for Jesus' sake, Amen."

Dr. Cliff R. Johnson
From "Area of Concern," sermon delivered at Westminster Presbyterian Church in Alexandria, Virginia on January 5, 1964

INTRODUCTION

In 1939, two men—Samuel W. Tucker and the Rev. Frederick W. Haverkamp—put into motion a series of events that would have a lasting impact on the city of Alexandria, Virginia.

On August 21 of that year, Alexandria attorney Samuel Tucker led a group of five young Black men in a peaceful sit-in at the Alexandria Library on Queen Street, an action that Tucker hoped would create a test case to challenge the library's racial segregation policy. Even though the five men were quietly reading books inside the library, they were escorted out of the library by police and arrested for disorderly conduct, charges that were later dismissed.

In the aftermath of this action, the city hastily opened a "separate but equal" branch "for Negroes only," stocked with used and cast-off books. Samuel Tucker refused the invitation to apply for a library card to the Robinson Library on Wythe Street (now the Alexandria Black History Museum).

It would be another quarter century before Blacks were allowed full access to the same public facilities in Alexandria as whites. Nevertheless, the library sit-in is one of the nation's earliest examples of how nonviolent protest became an effective tool against racial segregation.[1]

Also in the summer of 1939, the Potomac Presbytery secured funds from the sale of church property in Little Washington, Virginia, to build a new church on the expanding western edge of Alexandria. A Northern Presbyterian pastor-evangelist named

---

1 Patricia Sullivan, "Lawyer Samuel Tucker and his Historic 1939 Sit-in at Segregated Alexandria Library," *Washington Post*, August 7, 2014, https://www.washingtonpost.com/local/lawyer-samuel-tucker-and-his-historic-1939-sit-in-at-segregated-alexandria-library/2014/08/05/c9c1d38e-1be8-11e4-ae54-0cfe1f974f8a_story.html

Frederick Haverkamp was tapped to be the organizing minister of the new church.[2]

Haverkamp went door-to-door in the neighborhood handing out flyers and talking to residents. The first services were held in December 1939 in a classroom at St. Agnes School, but worship was soon relocated to Haverkamp's home on Virginia Avenue.

The following December, 38 charter members of Haverkamp's new congregation met at George Mason School to organize the church that they named Westminster. The first members were Baptists, Methodists, and Congregationalists in addition to Presbyterians, and they transferred their memberships from churches in Alexandria, Charlottesville, Barboursville, and Gordonsville, Virginia; Arizona, Georgia, Maine, Maryland, Massachusetts, North Dakota, Pennsylvania, Ohio, Oklahoma, Tennessee, Washington State, and Washington, D.C.

According to the new member form, "The only requirement for membership is faith in the Lord Jesus Christ as your personal Saviour with all this implies—repentance, conversion, acknowledgment, serving."[3] While there's no indication that Blacks were ever explicitly barred from joining Westminster,[4] Blacks were not allowed to purchase or rent homes in many of the new middle-class neighborhoods that were developing west of Old Town during this period. A newspaper advertisement from 1940 with the heading "Go to Church Sunday" lists Westminster and services at the Haverkamp residence, but Black churches in the city, such as Bethel Presbyterian Church—founded in 1926 and the first Black church in the Potomac Presbytery—were not included in the listing.

As it remains today, the Westminster congregation consisted of many federal government and military officials and their families. A prime example was Major General Harry Vaughn, who served as a White House aide to President Harry Truman and was a Westminster member from 1944 until his death in 1981.

---

2 Haverkamp was also the organizing pastor of Trinity Church Arlington in the early 1940s when Arlington County was the fastest-growing county in the U.S. According to William E. Thompson, "The fact that a Northern Presbyterian pastor-evangelist was the residential organizer of both of these new wartime churches helped to dispel some of the lingering suspicions among the Potomac Presbytery brethren that very little good could possibly come out of the Northern Presbyterian Church."

3 The membership form included a pledge to "give fifty cents a week toward the building of the first unit of the new church being built on Cameron Mills Road." That building (which is now the Chapel and Johnson Parlor) opened on February 15, 1942.

4 Beverley Hills Community Church (now Beverley Hills Community United Methodist Church) was founded a year earlier than Westminster and was "open to all races and religions." See *Washington Post*, May 17, 2011, https://www.washingtonpost.com/local/obituaries/william-e-basom-pastor-of-alexandria-church/2011/05/14/AFVFX45G_story.html

The proposed new sanctuary for Westminster Presbyterian Church, 1951

Unquestionably, both the city and commonwealth in which Westminster was fashioned were still deeply and overtly racist. Remnants of Jim Crow laws remained in place. In 1940, Black Alexandrians taking a bus into D.C. had to sit in the rear of the bus until after it had crossed the 14th Street bridge. On the return trip, they would be compelled to move to a seat in the back as the bus entered Virginia.[5] A "very large" segment of Alexandria's Black population—which accounted for one-fifth of the city's total population—were domestic workers for white residents.[6] It was likely not until July 26, 1948, when President Truman issued an executive order to end segregation in the Armed Services, that some of Westminster's earliest members first experienced anything resembling integration.

Over the years, Westminster has attracted members who worked both in the public sphere and privately behind the scenes to improve race relations and to advance racial equity. One notable example was Carlyle "Connie" Ring, who is the subject of Part II. It wasn't until the 1970s that the church began to devote meaningful financial resources toward organizations serving people of color in the community and in the world (Part III).

---

5 Maurine McLaughlin, "The City Still Faces South a Century After Civil War," *Washington Post*, June 26, 1969, G1.

6 Ibid.

Dr. Cliff Johnson in his study at Westminster Presbyterian Church

PART I
THE CLIFF JOHNSON ERA

A 27-year-old named Clifford Ross Johnson arrived in Alexandria in 1943 as Westminster's first called pastor after a short stint at Leesburg (Va.) Presbyterian Church. A native of Columbus, Ga., he graduated from Presbyterian College in Clinton, S.C., earned a master's degree in journalism from the University of South Carolina, and then attended Union Theological Seminary in Richmond, Va. He was a fan of the Washington Senators, "Peanuts" cartoons, sailing, animals, and public schools. He was not a fan of Roman Catholicism, though he valued and sought out opportunities throughout his career for interfaith dialogue.

Filling the Pews

Johnson quickly made an impression in Alexandria. Westminster was adding new members so fast that it soon outgrew its new building and began building a larger sanctuary in 1952.[7] He was in demand as a board member and speaker for community organizations, and he substituted for the U.S. House of Representative's chaplain just five months after starting at Westminster. "The ever-affable, caring-to-a-fault Cliff Johnson was the virtual pastor to the entire city of Alexandria, and bankers and real estate agents and lawyers trusted his word," according to William E. Thompson, who authored a history of the Potomac Presbytery.[8]

Johnson's sermon style was plain-spoken and direct. He often warned the congregation in advance when they were about to hear something with which they might disagree, and he frequently acknowledged the risk of ostracizing members of the congregation.

---

[7] President Harry Truman gave an address at the cornerstone laying on November 23, 1952.

[8] William E. Thompson, "'A Set of Rebellious Scoundrels': Three Centuries of Presbyterians Along the Potomac" (Rockville, Md.: National Capital Presbytery, 1989), 276.

> From several previous sermons I have preached on our relationship with the Negro race and from my conversations with you, I know firsthand that within this congregation there is seemingly every possible shade of attitude towards this pressing and critical question [school integration]. It makes me confident that there is no single statement that I can make, therefore, on this matter that would meet the approval of every member of the congregation.[9]

> I shall try—I shall try to keep my personal bias concealed, and where my bias shows through, please forgive me. For those of you for whom my position is untenable, please try to keep from reacting in such a way as to refuse to accept other things I have to say.[10]

> I rather expect many of you to disagree with me. Some of you may even disagree quite strongly. It may even be that most of you will disagree. Be that as it may, please hear me out and then make up your own minds.[11]

Johnson believed that it was his duty as a pastor to share his personal convictions with the congregation.

> You will insist, I believe, that [associate pastor] Jim [Lundquist] and I preach our convictions, whatever they may be, whatever we believe to be God's will and you will reserve the right to agree or disagree.[12]

> I feel responsible always to proclaim my convictions on any issue that has to do with our position as Christians and citizens in America. I do not feel that you are under any obligation always to agree with me.[13]

> ... I could not very well live with the fact that at some future time people would look back and see what was transpiring at Westminster the Sunday after so much had been going on in our nation for a week and to find out that the minister

---

[9] Dr. Cliff R. Johnson, "Law of the Land," sermon delivered at Westminster Presbyterian Church, Alexandria, Va. on May 23, 1954.

[10] Dr. Cliff R. Johnson, "On These We Agree," sermon delivered at Westminster Presbyterian Church, Alexandria, Va. on September 7, 1958.

[11] Dr. Cliff R. Johnson, "When Children Pray," sermon delivered at Westminster Presbyterian Church, Alexandria, Va. on May 10, 1964.

[12] Johnson, "On These We Agree."

[13] Johnson, "When Children Pray."

hadn't even been reading the paper, or didn't know what was going on, or didn't care.["]14

Likewise, he believed that it was the duty of individual Christians to make informed judgments about the controversial questions of the day: "Every area of political concern is an area of <u>Christian</u> concern, and as a Christian you have a responsibility to make up your mind about the poll tax, whether you are for it or against it."15 He explained earlier in this sermon, delivered six months before President Lyndon Johnson signed the Civil Rights Act of 1964 into law, that he was opposed to the poll tax because "I feel like it is designed to limit the electorate, and there are some other very fine friends within the sound of my voice who are strongly for it, and that's perfectly all right."16

Dr. Cliff Johnson

Speaking Freely and Frankly

Johnson was passionate about "freedom of the pulpit," and grateful to Westminster church for giving him that freedom. He acknowledged that this was a luxury that many of his seminary classmates who headed churches in the south did not enjoy.17

> I urge this church to do in the future as it has done in the past, thank God, and that is to maintain complete freedom of the pulpit. I will put this congregation up against any congregation that I have ever seen or heard of in this particular

---

14 Dr. Cliff R. Johnson, "Making My Position Clear," sermon delivered at Westminster Presbyterian Church, Alexandria, Va. on March 14, 1965, a week after the "Bloody Sunday" protests in Selma, Ala.

15 Johnson, "Area of Concern."

16 Ibid.

17 Johnson, "Making My Position Clear."

THE 1950s

Congressional Prayer

Dr. Cliff Johnson gave the opening prayer for the U.S. Senate on May 25, 1953:

❝ ...Help us as a people, and as legislators, O God, to remember that the moral heights we have painfully climbed may be maintained only as in humility we call upon thee. ❞

And also for the U.S. House of Representatives on May 12, 1959:

❝ ...Grant that all that transpires within this Chamber this day may serve to make for understanding, for compassion, for brotherhood, and for peace. ❞

---

regard. From this pulpit I have always felt perfectly free to say whatever I believed to be God's will... God grant that the prophets of this church shall never be throttled in their proclamation of what they believe to be God's will, however wrong their convictions may be. When you have throttled the Protestant pulpit, you have killed the Protestant Church.[18] ❞

❝ ...It *is* one of my great convictions that the pulpit must be free—and that your minister must feel always not only free, but supported, to say whatever he believes to be God's will. And it is your obligation to support him in his freedom to proclaim that word, whether you agree with a particular position or not.[19] ❞

Nevertheless, he didn't always enthusiastically embrace preaching about race relations. Before his March 14, 1965, sermon on the events that had transpired a week earlier in Selma, Alabama, he allowed that he "postponed this decision until the very last minute trying to find some way to get out of it." He described himself as "in a very foul humor" and "very waspish disposition." He was clearly angry about the deadly violence inflicted upon the demonstrators, but he was also angry that the Protestant Church in the south was not getting the credit he thought it deserved to advance racial reconciliation.[20]

❝ It is my aim this morning to make everybody mad in due time, so if you find out that you're angry to start with, well just sit still; if you're not mad, why sit still, and I'll get to all of you before we're through.[21] ❞

And he concluded that worship service with the following:

---

18 Ibid.
19 Johnson, "When Children Pray."
20 Ibid.
21 Johnson, "Making My Position Clear."

> ...If you want to hear any more talk about the racial issue in the next few weeks, you're going to have to go somewhere else, because I'm not going to talk about it anymore for a spell, so if this happens to suit you, why come back; if it doesn't suit you, why see if you can find some other place to go, because I ain't going to be talking about it.[22]

Confronting Racism

Johnson's sermon following the May 17, 1954, *Brown v. Board of Education* decision from the Supreme Court that ruled that racial segregation in public schools was unconstitutional was one of his first to address the topic of race directly. He believed that the adverse reaction to the ruling among whites centered on three issues: 1. the possibility of intermarriage; 2. the erosion of residential segregation and resultant declining home values; and 3. the loss of special privilege and position. And he admitted that these issues were difficult for him personally.[23]

> What does the Bible have to say about intermarriage? That's easy—it doesn't have anything to say at all. There is absolutely no biblical basis for denying intermarriage... Does this mean that I am in favor of intermarriage. Not at all; it means that ultimately I am neither for nor against... With my own training and background I find even the idea revulsive and distasteful... It was my privilege to marry whom I pleased, whether my family liked it or not. I insist that the same right belongs to my children... I would be extremely disappointed, more than I would be heartbroken for one of my children to marry a Roman Catholic....
>
> As far as my feelings go, I would not want Negroes moving into the neighborhood. I would not want my investment threatened. I would not want to suffer the cultural penalty of being identified with a mixed racial neighborhood... Those are my feelings—but, because they are my feelings, that does not mean that they are right—that does not mean they are Christian—it doesn't even mean that they are

---

22 Ibid.

23 Johnson, "Law of the Land."

> sound. Those are my feelings, but believe you me, I'm not proud of them, and I don't propose to try to defend them… I have to wrestle with my feelings, and that I propose to do….
>
> Dealing with the emotions long and deeply engendered in us will not be easy; but our duty and responsibility as American citizens and as individual Christians is quite clear. I charge you as fellow Christians to rise to meet the challenge. Not only as Christians do I charge you, but particularly as Presbyterians. Our Presbyterian theology, built upon the sovereignty of God, furnished the very life blood out of which American freedom originally sprang… We can be proud but not surprised that within 48 hours of the Supreme Court pronouncement, Dr. Frank Price, Moderator of the General Assembly of the Presbyterian Church in the United States spoke out to say, 'This ruling was necessary, wise and right—a ringing affirmation of our American faith in liberty and equality.' Because of my own decrepit little soul, it may well be that frequently I shall be uncomfortable, but as a Christian and a Presbyterian I dare not do otherwise than stand up and declare, praise God, let freedom ring.[24]

Johnson also responded from the pulpit to events happening close to home. The "Massive Resistance" effort by U.S. Senator Harry F. Byrd Sr. and his son, State Senator Harry F. Byrd Jr., to block school integration flourished in Alexandria, where the elder Byrd's cousin, Marshall J. Beverley, was mayor in the 1950s. Tensions rose in September 1958 after 14 Black students in Alexandria filed suit in U.S. District Court to transfer to white schools. School superintendent T.C. Williams fired school cafeteria worker Blois Hundley for joining the lawsuit on behalf of her children. A few days later Williams reversed the firing under the threat of a civil rights investigation by the Justice Department, which Beverley characterized as the action of "a Gestapo and dictatorial government."[25]

In October 1958, after Temple Beth El Rabbi Emmet Frank condemned the "Byrd political oligarchy" and Virginia's resistance to school integration during a Yom Kippur sermon and was promptly criticized by local officials, a group of 11 Protestant

---

24 Ibid.

25 "Beverley Charges 'Gestapo' Tactics in School Dispute," *Alexandria Gazette*, October 4, 1958, 1.

ministers in Alexandria, including Johnson, wrote a letter in support of Frank.[26] They wrote, "Certainly one of the strongest convictions held jointly by Jews and Christians is that religion divorced from daily life is meaningless ceremony. Church and temple, minister and rabbi, must endeavor to speak to the deepest needs of people in their personal lives and in their community relationships."[27]

In the midst of the turmoil, on September 7, 1958, Johnson preached about "the question of the integration of the public schools now upon our very own doorstep," which he described as the most critical issue that the Christian Church had faced since the Civil War. He deliberately avoided presenting his own position, though he allowed that his position was "practically that of all of the other Protestant ministers, rabbis and priests in this community" (i.e., supportive of integration).[28]

His message to the congregation was to stand together in support of an orderly transition and to stand against violence and name-calling.

> We must have freedom in this church to talk among ourselves, to disagree among ourselves, to feel our way toward what we believe to be God's will....
>
> First, all of us can ask God to give us loving, forgiving hearts; we can ask God to give us His guidance and the courage to do His will... Second, all of us can and must pray

---

26 Ibid.

27 An earlier paragraph in the letter states that "our concern at this point is not the substance of the sermon, but rather the two other issues of (1) Jewish-Christian relations and (2) separation of church and state which have been raised subsequently."

28 Thompson says that "Potomac Presbytery was widely regarded all throughout the Southern Presbyterian Church as being an exceedingly 'liberal' body, and most especially was this true in matters relating to challenging segregation and in actively promoting racial integration...Its white pastors tended to be somewhat idealistic, visionary persons, and its white lay leaders had had considerable experience in relating to black persons as peers in the government milieu, where issues of equality had been faced earlier than in the Church."

1960

The *Alexandria Gazette* published an article written by Dr. Cliff Johnson on February 20, 1960. The topic was Brotherhood Week.

> *...Protestants, Roman Catholics, Greek Orthodox, Hebrews, members of other religious groups and pagans all breathe America's free air. Representatives of each of these groups dissent profoundly from each other's religious or non-religious point of view. No one in his right mind ever aims at reducing religion to a common denominator. Thus reduced it is at best pious platitudes and at worst moralistic mockery.... Among ourselves we shall continue to disagree on many things, even at times to the point of anger, but even in the midst of our emotions we shall maintain our universal commitment to freedom and democracy. This means a willingness on the part of every man to accept responsibilities commensurate with his privileges and to accord to every other man the same privileges and to expect of him no greater responsibilities. While we are getting around to coining slogans, it's still hard to beat the one which says, 'Let freedom ring,' and <u>that should make all of us ardent members of the Freedom Bell Ringers Union, whatever our race, color or creed.</u>*

for the community—that God will help this community to find a way to resolve this problem in peace, love, and harmony. Third, we must pray for those who have a different position from our own....

Our love for each other which binds us together must be a testimony to the world that the love of Christ which is in our hearts is so powerful that <u>no issue</u>, whatever its nature, can tear us apart.[29] ""

On March 14, 1965, exactly a week after "Bloody Sunday"—the protest against Black voter suppression in Selma at which civil rights marchers were brutally beaten and attacked by police[30]—Johnson preached one of his most powerful sermons about racism.

"" The matter of Negro voter registration in Selma <u>is</u> a moral issue. Hence, it does concern the Christian conscience. When human beings are wronged, discriminated against, or used in any fashion other than as free human beings, then a Christian has no choice but to act upon that which is taking place....

I say without equivocation that the day must end when being a Negro in the South makes one a second-class citizen. As a Christian, and as a minister, I must contend for the end of segregation in the church, in the schools, in the business and the political life of the South....

There have been some people in this church who have felt like I have compromised on this matter of my position regarding segregation and integration, regarding the role of the Negro in this church and in this community, regarding my feelings about what should be the Negro's rights in our nation. I have just spoken my piece as clearly as I know how.[31] ""

Confessing His Own Prejudices

Johnson acknowledged numerous times from the pulpit how difficult it was for him

---

29 Johnson, "On These We Agree."

30 According to Thompson, "Quite a number of Potomac Presbytery laity and clergy joined the thousands of religious people from across the nation who journeyed to Selma."

31 Johnson, "Making My Position Clear."

personally to confront the issue of race, and how he continually asked for God's help to avoid giving in to "feelings that are loaded with prejudice, resentment and dislike."[32] Having been raised amid white privilege in Georgia, he was reared to treat Blacks kindly—and paternalistically—and in return Blacks treated him with deference, even as a youngster.[33]

> It was assumed by my parents and by other adults who surrounded me that they and I were better than Negroes; we were more intelligent, we were more capable, and we were more able. It never crossed my mind that anyone seriously considered Negroes equal to white people—nor did it ever cross the minds of the Negroes with whom I was associated. In looking back I had no feelings of guilt about all this; this is just the way it was....
>
> What has brought about my change in feeling about the Negroes? Several things, but basically I find myself disliking them because they now insist on rocking my delightfully luxurious boat. Negroes don't want to treat me with deference anymore. They don't want to act and feel their inferiority to me; as a matter of fact, they want to insist on equality. I liked it so much better the other way. Surely the Negro doesn't expect me to like him as much this way as I did the other, when he was my obsequious, obedient, deferential servant, grateful for my paternal care. He no longer wants my paternal care—and hear these words—I do not blame him! Negroes now insist on being full human beings, full citizens with full dignity; this bothers me because it invades,

---

32 Dr. Cliff R. Johnson, "The Color of Tragedy," sermon delivered at Westminster Presbyterian Church, Alexandria, Va. on April 7, 1968.

33 Ibid.

1965

In a December 26, 1965, sermon directed to college students returning home for winter break, Dr. Cliff Johnson tells the story of two brilliant young physicists who gave a presentation to the Men's Club shortly after the end of WWII. Johnson chatted with them long after all of the others had left. Their car was parked in the George Mason school parking lot, and they cranked and cranked the engine until they were about to drain the battery. This anecdote—as related by Johnson himself—contains one of his more hurtful expressions on record but is included here to ensure that the record is not sanitized or incomplete.

> *I called down to Arlex Esso and I had them send—and I mention the fact that it was a colored boy only to make a point here in a moment—a colored lad up here. In just a few minutes, he arrived. He didn't even bother to try to start the car; he lifted the hood, took off the distributor cap, dried it out, put it back on, and got in the car, turned on the switch and started the car. So then the two young scientists drove off. The whole point being that I learned then never to be scornful of wisdom anywhere that it might be.*

upsets and disturbs my prerogatives and my prejudices and my position....

These are my deep and genuine feelings growing right out of my most deep laid emotional pattern... But I am now trying with the daily help of God—and believe me it takes that—not to live by my feelings but to live rather by my convictions, my intellect and my will. I think my feelings are wrong; I think they are not Christian... I will acknowledge them as I have just done, that those feelings are there, but I refuse to live by them.[34] "

In an April 9, 1967, sermon about loneliness and the fear of being rejected by other people and rejected by God, Johnson concluded with the following:[35]

" The other evening, I found myself sitting at a table at dinner, a circular table for ten people. And next to me was seated a Negro gentleman, the only Negro at the table. And really, much to my surprise, I found welling up within me old feelings of resentment and anger and rejection, with which I was reared, and I thought I had pretty well licked. There they were, welling up down inside. I found myself thinking about the conflicts in our Nation, and taking sides in my own feelings then, and tremendously stirred up. And all of a sudden I looked at this fellow and I started asking myself, 'I wonder how he feels.' I noticed that he was looking straight ahead and eating his dinner while everybody around the table was talking. I wondered how he felt being the only Negro, and nine white people, and all of this conversation going on of which he was no part, about his anxieties, his fears, his feelings of rejection, so all of a sudden I turned and I started talking to him. I was overwhelmed with the feelings which arose obviously from him of gratitude and response to my overtures.

That's no great thing... It didn't change anything, I guess—except me. I guess that's not so great—but maybe it is—maybe it is. "

---

34 Ibid.

35 Dr. Cliff R. Johnson, "The Tap Root," sermon delivered at Westminster Presbyterian Church, Alexandria, Va. on April 9, 1967.

Venturing Policy Prescriptions

Johnson also used his sermons to introduce some policy ideas that were forward-thinking—and controversial—for the times. In a May 10, 1964, sermon regarding Bible-reading and prayer in public schools, he described the Supreme Court decision to ban school-sponsored prayer as "wise and proper," an opinion that was shared by the Potomac Presbytery.[36]

> As Bible reading and prayer are generally conducted in the public schools…a Protestant Bible that is used, a Protestant version of the Lord's Prayer that is said, and therefore the practice discriminates against the Roman Catholics who are present, against the Jews, and against the non-believers. And as a Protestant, I do not want this situation corrected by our turning to having Jewish prayers or Roman Catholic emphases. Let me say parenthetically that I wonder how many of the thousands upon <u>thousands</u> of petitioners who are writing into their Congressmen—I wonder how many of them faithfully have Bible reading and prayer in their homes each day.…
>
> Whenever a minority group feels and demonstrates that there has been religious discrimination, then our court <u>must</u> draw the line between separation of church and state even sharper… For I am convinced that our Lord Jesus would not at any time have us use the power of a majority to superimpose on anyone what we believe should be our relationship with Him.[37]

His April 7, 1968, sermon in the days following the death of Martin Luther King Jr. included not only his distress and personal regret over "the violent, cowardly assassination of one of my fellow ministers," but also a call to action—"new ways of thinking, some new ways of evaluating and acting"—to address poverty in the inner cities. First, he advocated taking "a half or a fourth of the billions which we are now pouring

---

36 According to Thompson, "Some elders and pastors alike were outraged when the Presbytery voted that it found this decision to be absolutely consistent with its own understanding of the traditional church and state relationships in this country." The full Presbytery statement was: "We acknowledge that the promotion of the Christian gospel cannot and will not be accomplished in or through our public schools. Nor should it be. The Church and the Church alone can fulfill this function which God, through Christ, has ordained for it."

37 Johnson, "When Children Pray."

into this [Vietnam] war and use it to make tremendous inroads into the massive problem of our cities…They must know that society does care." Second, he called upon Christians to "use every iota of restraint, insight and intelligence that we have. We must do everything in our power first to understand." Lastly, "as Christians we have to use everything in our power to manifest restraint against our own counter feelings of hostility and resentment. For wherever as Christians we feel hatred we must wrestle with those feelings."[38]

In a sermon on "open housing" and integrated neighborhoods, Johnson asked a rhetorical question that 25 years later would become a popular slogan for wristbands and bracelets:

> As I try to have the courage to do whenever I face an area of either personal or social moral concern, I try to ask seriously and reflectively, 'What would Jesus do?' and 'What would Jesus have me to do?'[39]

His reply to his own question:

> I have envisioned having Jesus sitting in my study and in [my] imagination I have asked Him if I have the right as a Christian to decline to sell my home to a Negro because he is a Negro? Do I have a right as a Christian, either by passive resistance or active involvement, to keep Negroes out of my neighborhood because they are Negroes? I believe that Jesus would say to me that as a Christian I do not have that right. I must say in all honesty that I do not like that answer. I have feelings against Negroes living in my house or moving into my neighborhood, but I do not think those are Christian feelings and I do not think Jesus would condone them. Therefore, I am stuck with what I believe Jesus would say: as far as I am concerned, He is my boss and I can't go against what I believe He would say. In turn then, I have no choice but to favor open housing and to say that a community that calls itself Christian should voluntarily accept open housing.[40]

In the first sermon from a 1969 series about the Church and the world, Johnson

---

38 Johnson, "The Color of Tragedy."'
39 Dr. Cliff R. Johnson, "On Being Uncomfortable," sermon delivered at Westminster Presbyterian Church in Alexandria, Va. on February 26, 1968.
40 Ibid.

floated the idea of a universal basic income to lift people out of poverty and out of the ghetto.

> I'm not saying I'm in favor yet, but I'm saying I am ready to hear some more about a serious proposal to provide a minimum family income for every family in the country, including every family in the ghetto....
>
> I am herewith assuming my Christian responsibility to be willing to contribute to the solution directly wherever I have the wisdom and the fortitude and the commitment to do so—and indirectly wherever I can, through my government or my church.[41]

Associate Pastor John Watkins also addressed themes of racial and economic justice in his sermons during the late 1960s.

> ...We cannot preach that Christ breaks every barrier down between men and then go ahead and maintain those barriers of race, economics and social status. This is a contradiction in terms. And we cannot preach the justice of God, God's compassion for the needy and the downtrodden and the poverty-stricken, and then be unconcerned for those in poverty as they live their lives here in Alexandria, in our nation, and in the world.
>
> Jesus did not just talk about God's concern for the needs of men, he <u>was</u> concerned for the needs of men in this world. And this is the challenge then that is given to the Church in our day: to proclaim and to witness to our God who has chosen to be known by his actions in the very center of life,

---

[41] Dr. Cliff R. Johnson, "The Church and the Ghetto," sermon delivered at Westminster Presbyterian Church in Alexandria, Va. on March 9, 1969.

"A HOMILETIC ARTIST"

Copies of sermons given by Cliff Johnson, who was described by a *Washington Post* reporter as "a homiletic artist with a change of pace," were so often requested that two volumes of them were published by Westminster. *Jesus' Financial Troubles* is a collection of eight sermons that Johnson delivered between 1948 and 1953. The book was given to Johnson by the church in honor of his tenth anniversary as senior pastor. *Every Moment an Easter* contains a series of sermons delivered in 1962 on the Apostles' Creed and how each phrase had undergone changes in meaning during the various stages of Church history. Both books are available at the Pera Library at Westminster.

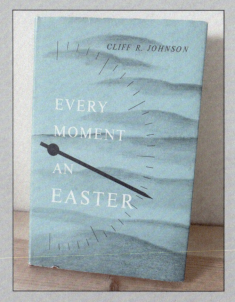

not just on the fringes of life, although as I've said he's there to be sure. But God wants to be known in the center of life. This is the meaning of the incarnation—that God assumes unto himself human life in all of its fullness.

Now there are healthy signs that the church has accepted the challenge, for the church is becoming as individuals and as a church more involved in the great social issues of our time. It _is_ wrestling with a new theology which seeks basically nothing more than to restate the ancient truths that God was in Christ reconciling the world unto himself but in the form that men will understand today. It _is_ seeking new forms of worship and new forms of ministry to the secular city in which we live. We have picked up the challenge but now it remains for all of us to commit ourselves wholeheartedly to follow our Lord who acts in the center of life, in the midst of life, the God we see in Jesus Christ, and to follow him wherever he leads us wherever that may be.[42]

One realm where Johnson refrained from delivering personal viewpoints from the pulpit was endorsements of political candidates. But he nevertheless made himself available on a Sunday evening, January 31, 1960, in Fellowship Hall to share his views regarding a Catholic presidential candidate, and he sent a memo to the congregation inviting them to attend.

With our nation being confronted with the declared candidacy for the presidency by a member of the Roman Catholic Church, each American must now deal with this issue according to his own conscience and convictions.

As a Christian, a Presbyterian, a minister and an American, I feel that all four of these roles require of me to make public my own convictions. By the same token, I feel that the pulpit of the church of which I am minister cannot be used legitimately for the presentation and resolution of such as issue. Therefore, I am choosing a Sunday evening in Fellowship Hall as the time and occasion for my presenting my views. This means that all who are interested may come and all

---

42 Rev. John M. Watkins, "I Am," sermon delivered at Westminster Presbyterian Church in Alexandria, Va. on April 2, 1967.

who are uninterested or have convictions which do not need to be reviewed can comfortably stay away. This will provide me with the freedom to speak my convictions, knowing that I am speaking to people who have deliberately chosen to come, with a full awareness of the topic to be discussed.[43]

There is sparse evidence that Johnson's views on integration, racial justice and other hot-button issues of mid-20th century offended members to the point of driving them away from the church. Westminster grew rapidly during most of the time that Johnson was senior pastor and reached its membership peak of 2,100 members in 1965, five years before his death.[44] He frequently acknowledges offending listeners on both sides of the political divide, including during the sermon that he preached following the assassination of Martin Luther King Jr.

> My decisions to speak and not to speak on social issues have had their effect on the membership and outlook of this church. On the one hand we have lost a little cluster of capable members who could not tolerate this church any longer because they felt that I was not aggressive enough in declaring my position on social issues. At the other end of the spectrum, we have lost a little cluster of members who have felt me to be too determined to sound off on things which in their judgment were not the legitimate concern of the church.[45]

One week following the Sunday when he preached about Selma (in a sermon titled "Making My Position Clear"), Johnson prefaced his sermon by acknowledging the positive and supportive response he had received from members of the congregation.

> I should like to make a brief commentary about last Sunday's sermon. For those of you who heard it, I want to assure you that you can sleep quietly this morning, for the most consequential thing that I intend to say has to do with my being in favor of motherhood, righteousness, and the American flag. I want to say seriously that I'm grateful for and humbled by the rather flood of letters of

---

43 Memorandum from Dr. Cliff R. Johnson to the Westminster Presbyterian Church congregation, "Romanism and the Presidency," January 25, 1960.

44 According to Session minutes from December 13, 1967, the membership rolls were purged of inactive members, reducing the number of active members by about 400 people at the end of that year.

45 Johnson, "The Color of Tragedy."

commendation and support which I have received and the plethora of telephone calls and the number of people who stopped me in the course of the week on the street, here at the church and elsewhere. And by the same token I would like to express my appreciation for the gracious and silent restraint of those who may have disagreed with me very strongly.⁴⁶ "

Foreseeing the Future

Johnson perhaps had a sense that the comings-and-goings of members over this or that controversy were far less significant than the legacy that Westminster would leave for the years to come. In his 1958 sermon on school integration, he presciently envisaged that future generations would seek to know where Westminster stood during his tenure as senior pastor.

" Someday this cloud is going to pass. I do not know whether it will be two years, five years, ten years or fifty years—but some day the cloud will pass. This issue will have been resolved—the storm will clear, the skies will brighten. And then history will be written. Somebody will go back and write what was done in this community in this conflict. It is my unabashed aim, as the minister of this church, for Westminster to have one glowing page in that book. I should like for that page which shall be written in history about the conduct of Westminster to run something like this: There was a bitter struggle in that community; there were high feelings, there was anger and there were internal conflicts throughout the community. The bitterness and the feelings ran into one crisis after another, but right on through the battle, there was a church known as Westminster Church which in her unity stood solidly as a rock.

Oh, there were feelings in the church, there were differences of opinion and sometimes the feelings would begin to run too high. Just when the battle was the hottest, just when it would appear that a break was inevitable, someone would stand up and shout, "Christ is King." Across the field of battle would echo the

---

46 Dr. Cliff R. Johnson, "Calendars, Sacred and Secular," sermon delivered at Westminster Presbyterian Church in Alexandria, Va. on March 21, 1965.

Dr. Cliff Johnson

voice, "Christ is King, Christ is King," and then all hands would be joined, all hearts would be made tender, and Westminster would stand shoulder to shoulder to face the world."[47]

Johnson's sermons represent not only a rare and personal window into a human being who struggled mightily with his deeply entrenched feelings about race and white privilege, but also a treatise on how his understanding of his Christian faith and Christ's example guided the evolution of his viewpoints on issues related to race during his too-short career. His congregants no doubt were wrestling with the same moral questions, and thousands of Westminster members during the Cliff Johnson era sought out his insight and guidance. "He packs his church every Sunday with people who come to be surprised, stirred, lifted and brought closer to what they feel in their bones is ultimate truth," wrote *Washington Post* staff reporter Kenneth Dole in 1959.[48]

When he died from a brain tumor in February 1970 just a month shy of 54 years old, the *Alexandria Gazette* described Johnson as someone who could "transfer a message of religious impact and uplift without seeming to give a sermon"[49] and wrote that "he strove for better understanding between denominations, particularly Catholic and Protestant, and between the black and white races."[50]

---

47 Johnson, "On These We Agree."

48 Kenneth Dole, "Sermons with Humor Draw Flock to Church," *Washington Post*, March 7, 1959, D7.

49 "There Was a Man...," *Alexandria Gazette*, February 11, 1970.

50 "Dr. Johnson, Westminster, Dies at 53," *Alexandria Gazette*, February 6, 1970.

Connie Ring in front of T.C. Williams High School, now named Alexandria City High School, in 2011
Photo by Steven Halperson/Tisara Photography

PART II
CONNIE RING: FAITH IN ACTION IN THE COMMUNITY

Cliff Johnson's "absolutely fabulous" preaching was one of the many reasons that the young newlyweds, Jane and Carlyle "Connie" Ring, chose to join Westminster in 1957. It was close to their Parkfairfax home and "it was very friendly and had lots of young couples and families," says Jane.

The Rings had arrived in Alexandria a year earlier, after Connie had graduated from Duke University Law School. Jane had to return to Durham, North Carolina for a semester to finish up her degree at Duke, so their search for a church home didn't begin in earnest until 1957. "We walked into Westminster and immediately felt at home and knew we were meant to be there," adds Jane.

Connie was born with an appreciation for public education in his DNA. His father was superintendent of Jamestown, New York public schools, his mother and sister were both teachers in public schools, and his two brothers spent their careers in higher education. Connie was the exception—the only non-education professional in his family.

As a volunteer with Legal Aid in Durham during law school, Connie provided legal assistance to Black residents in parts of the city where the streets were not even paved. This experience gave him a first-hand look at racial discrimination. "For a white kid from upstate New York, it was eye-opening," says Jane.

Early Interest in Public Service

Connie believed every child deserved a quality public education and that such training was "the great equalizer" of racial and socio-economic inequities. So it's no surprise that when he arrived in Alexandria in 1956, he adamantly opposed the "Massive Resistance" against school integration that was prevalent in Alexandria and across the state of Virginia.

Connie Ring In the 1970s

One of Connie's first errands as a new Alexandria resident was to register to vote for the 1956 Presidential election. During the Byrd era, the Senator and his machine had successfully limited the size of the electorate—voter participation averaged 12%. State restrictions that were enacted in 1902 were still in place: a poll tax of $1.50 paid in each of the previous three years; and "blank sheet" registration that required the applicant to answer a series of questions in writing under oath on a blank piece of paper.[51] When he was handed a blank piece of paper, Connie became infuriated and asked the election official, "What would you have done for a Black?"[52] Connie promptly sued the Board of Elections, which resulted in a standardized registration form.

Connie and Jane became involved in the community and at Westminster church almost immediately. Connie served on the Parks and Recreation Commission and the North Ridge Citizens' Association. He and Jane were youth leaders at Westminster starting in 1957. One outing they planned for the church youth was a picnic with a group of Black kids from Junior Village, a home for homeless children located in southwest D.C. A rainstorm forced the Rings to relocate the picnic to Fellowship Hall. A fellow member was arranging flowers in the kitchen and lodged a complaint with Cliff Johnson, who apparently took no action.

As chair of the Alexandria Republican party from 1961 to 1968, Connie further developed his reputation for activism, seeking to find middle ground between the two prevailing political forces in the city—the Byrd wing of the Democratic party and the more progressive Democrats. He worked to create voter registration sites outside of city government buildings, reduce the one-year residency requirement for voting and eliminate the state poll tax.[53]

---

51 Election officials used the "blank sheet" registration method to deny registration to those who weren't literate, didn't answer the correct questions in the right order or misspelled words.

52 Living Legends of Alexandria, https://alexandrialegends.org/carlyle-connie-ring/

53 Even after the 24th Amendment was passed in 1962 outlawing the poll tax, Virginia was one of five states that maintained the voting requirement, along with Alabama, Arkansas, Mississippi, and Texas. It remained in place until 1965 when the federal government had to sue the state to abolish it. Even as recently as 1976, Virginia ranked last among states in the percentage of population registered to vote.

Forming Key Alliances

Connie became close friends with Rev. Joseph Penn of Alexandria's Third Baptist Church (a historically Black church) when the two of them worked together to reach out to labor groups and Black voters on behalf of Linwood Holton's 1965 gubernatorial campaign. When D.C. erupted into riots following the MLK assassination, Rev. Penn contacted Connie. Concerned about possible disturbances in Alexandria, Rev. Penn asked Connie to enlist some of his white friends and neighbors to join him and a group of Black residents at the Alexandria courthouse as a show of unity and calm. Connie did so; in all, about 50 or 60 people showed up.

In 1969 Rev. Penn gave a presentation to the men's group at Westminster about the challenges facing Blacks living in ghettos. Members of both churches together organized several fundraising events, including a concert by the Howard University Gospel Choir at Alexandria City High School[54] on March 1, 1970. The concert raised the equivalent of about $16,000 in 2022 dollars, funds that were used to start a day care center at a low-income housing project on N. Payne Street, support the "adoption" of families in need, and underwrite the operation of mobile health unit facilities.

According to the concert program:

> Our two congregations have undertaken this joint effort as a living demonstration that two races can work together for constructive purposes on a full parity basis in this time when the world seems to be saying that this is no longer possible. We feel that this joint demonstration of unity is particularly essential at this time after the tensions of last fall.

Connie endeavored to form close, personal relationships with other Black leaders in the city. He and Jane hosted a monthly breakfast of Black leaders at their home just down the hill from Westminster that was attended by Ferdinand Day,[55] Melvin Miller,[56] Helen Miller, Nelson Greene, Ruby Tucker and Gene Tucker, among others.

---

54 Formerly T.C. Williams High School.

55 Ferdinand Day, who was appointed to the Alexandria School Board in 1964, was the first Black school board chair in the state of Virginia.

56 Melvin Miller was part of the biracial commission appointed by Alexandria Mayor Leroy Bendheim in June 1960 to help bring about an orderly desegregation of department store lunch counters in the city.

In 2014, Living Legends of Alexandria celebrated the 50th anniversary of the Civil Rights Act by honoring leaders who were active in Alexandria civil rights during the 1960s. Pictured (front row, left to right): Ferdinand Day, Nelson Greene Sr. Back row: Connie Ring, Gwendolyn "Peggy" Menefee-Smith, former Va. state senator Patsy Ticer, former Alexandria mayor William Euille, Melvin Miller

Photo by Steven Halperson/Tisara Photography

At the Center of the City's Struggle Toward School Integration

In 1969 a city council that was composed of five Democrats and two Republicans appointed Connie Ring to the school board, the first Republican appointed to that body in Alexandria's history. These were tense times to be a public official. In May 1970, a Black teenager was shot and killed by a white 7-Eleven store manager at the corner of Commonwealth Avenue and West Glebe Road. Six nights of rioting and firebombing followed. In November 1970, a group of 20 white youth and men burned a cross in front of George Washington High School,[57] where 25% of the students were Black, and school superintendent John Albohm's house was picketed by members of the American Nazi Party. Another white-only organization, the Alexandria Citizens Defense League, took it upon themselves to patrol the streets.[58]

---

57 Now George Washington Middle School.

58 Dr. Krystyn Moon, "Alexandria in 1969: Police Violence, Race Relations, and a Call for Reform," Office of Historic Alexandria.

School integration was the defining—and most divisive—issue for the school board during Connie's tenure. By the late 1960s, there was only token desegregation in some of the schools.[59] In May 1971 the school division adopted a secondary school reorganization that integrated upper grades but kept the existing elementary school structure intact. The "6-2-2-2" plan was favored by Superintendent Albohm, who unlike his predecessor, T.C. Williams, was more of a pragmatist rather than an obstructionist when it came to integration.[60]

When school reconvened that fall under the new plan, Connie and Richard B. Hills, an assistant school superintendent, stood outside of Hammond High School[61] to greet the buses. They escorted Black students inside the building to prevent white parents from throwing rocks at them. (Prior to this time, Hammond, with a student body of 1,547, had two Black students and no Black teachers.)

The 6-2-2-2 plan, however, did not address the growing segregation of elementary schools on the east side of the city, and Alexandria City Public Schools (ACPS) was again informed by the federal Department of Health, Education and Welfare's (HEW) regional civil rights director that it did not comply with current law, thus threatening federal funding. Albohm pledged to HEW Civil Rights Director J. Stanley Pottinger that ACPS would come up with a plan so that no elementary school would have a majority of Black students. Any plan would inevitably involve busing young students around the city.[62]

According to the ACPS website pages that document the school division's history:

> The rumor that elementary schools were about to be desegregated brought crowds out to the March 1972 school board meeting opposing the change. The George Mason PTA president said 95 percent of its members were against

---

59 As an illustration of Alexandria's obstinacy to school desegregation, in the city of Birmingham, Ala.—regarded as the most segregated city in the U.S. at the time—twenty students integrated its white schools in 1963. It was school integration in Birmingham that provoked the September 16, 1963, bombing of 16th Street Baptist Church, which killed four young girls and marked a turning point in the civil rights movement.

60 "6-2-2-2" was shorthand for the existing K-6 elementary school structure; two neighborhood-based junior high schools for grades 7 and 8; two existing high schools for grades 9 and 10; and all 11th and 12th grade students attending T. C. Williams High School.

61 Now Francis Hammond Middle School.

62 Seventy percent of Alexandria's Black elementary students attended five schools on the east end of the city.

> busing and described the school as the equivalent of a church: 'the center of neighborhood activities.' Albohm backed down and said he would no longer bus students across the city.
>
> The dispute over elementary busing to try to desegregate the schools caused the conservative city council, who appointed the school board members, to flex their political muscle. They replaced the liberal members who supported desegregation of the elementary schools with conservatives.[63]

The city council replaced two departing school board members (including Ferdinand Day) with busing opponents, but they reappointed Connie, who had initially opposed busing for elementary school students. Numerous plans were put forth by Albohm and school board members who were attempting to thread the needle between white opponents of busing and the prospect of court-ordered busing if the school board failed to act. (HEW had already begun the process to cut off federal funding.)

In May 1973, Connie offered a compromise plan that would pair eight elementary schools and require busing of approximately 3,000 students. A predominantly white school was paired with a predominantly Black school; students would attend one of the paired schools for the lower grades and the other paired school for the upper grades. Jane describes as "scary" the angry letters that Connie received from constituents opposed to the busing plan.

Connie ultimately voted against the final version of the compromise which the school board passed with a 5-4 vote; he favored his original version that was less expensive and required fewer children to be bused, but which placed more of the burden of busing on Black children. Jane recalls that Connie told fellow school board member Bill Hurd that "if you are not careful you will resegregate the city because families will move out of the city or transfer to private schools."

As Connie predicted, white parents expressed their displeasure by voting with their feet. In the summer of 1974, more than 900 families moved out of Alexandria or enrolled their children in private schools. By 1976, the number of white children attending ACPS had fallen by half compared to what it had been in 1970.

---

63 "Brown v. Board: 60 Years On – The Action that Took 14 Years to Complete," Alexandria City Public Schools, February 2, 2019, http://www.acpsk12.org/news/?p=12150

Reaching Across Many Aisles

Connie was again reappointed to the school board in 1975 and served as chair from 1975 to 1978. During his school board years, Connie visited Black churches at least once a month. One of those churches was Ebenezer Baptist, where the Rev. Austin Booker had been on the school board with Connie and Ferdinand Day. During a sermon about loving one another that Connie attended, Rev. Booker asked the congregation to turn to the person next to them and kiss them on the cheek. It's not known who was more taken aback by this—Connie or the person sitting next to him.

In 1979 Connie was elected to the city council along with his friend Democrat Nelson Greene, who was the second Black to serve on the city council,[64] and he served for nearly a decade. In 1988 Connie made an unsuccessful bid for mayor against incumbent Democratic Mayor Jim Moran. Connie was also a member of the Alexandria Redevelopment and Housing Authority for 11 years.

Connie Ring receiving Hamilton College's Bell Ringer Award in 2015

Photo by Nancy L. Ford for Hamilton College

Connie, who died in August 2021 at the age 90, was one of many Westminster members who have held public office in Alexandria and served on city commissions. For a period of time in the early 1980s, five-term Democratic mayor Charles Beatley, and Republican city council members Robert Calhoun and Connie were all active members.[65] "I had to keep a little bit of peace with both sides," recalls Dr. George Pera, senior pastor at Westminster from 1980 to 1995.

Adds Winki Campbell, whose husband, the late Rev. Don Campbell, succeeded Johnson as senior pastor at Westminster, "It was people like Connie who stood firmly, but not aggressively, for what they believed in and set a beautiful example for everyone else."

---

64 Ira Robinson, elected in 1970, was the first.

65 In addition, Robert "Bob" Calhoun served in the Virginia State Senate from 1988 to 1996.

Dr. Cliff Johnson (left) and an elder of the church, Major General Harry Vaughn (right), look on as President Harry S Truman (center) lays the cornerstone of Westminster's new sanctuary in November 1952.

PART III
THE EVOLUTION OF WESTMINSTER'S CONGREGATION

For most of its first three decades, Westminster was growing by leaps and bounds. The church's two governing bodies, the Session and the Diaconate, were nearly single-mindedly focused on a recurring cycle of planning new construction, raising funds to pay for construction, managing construction, confronting new space constraints, planning more construction, and so forth.

From its founding, the church facility has been a hub of community activity. One of the city's oldest Scouts BSA troops, Troop 129, has been operating continuously since January 1941. As early as 1954, the brand-new sanctuary and fellowship hall were used by Temple Beth El for high holidays.

Presidential Visit

President Harry S Truman laid the cornerstone of the present sanctuary on November 23, 1952.[66] Along with pointing out that he had met his wife Bess at age six in Sunday School at his family's Presbyterian church, his remarks also called upon the nation's churches to hold up the standard for peace and justice and to point the way.

> Our churches must keep pace not only with the changes in our physical development, but also, and more importantly, with the changes of social problems. Our churches must not become a place to hide from the facts of the world about us, nor a mere badge of social responsibility. Too often our churches have been blind to their most important function, which is to bring about the application of religious principles to our daily lives and in our work. We must all wage a ceaseless war against injustice in our society. The churches in particular are a force which

---

66 An eight-minute video recording of the event is at
https://www.youtube.com/watch?v=ibw0lZFzamc

WESTMINSTER'S FIRST "FIRST LADY"

Ona Winants Borland Haverkamp was a full partner in the work of her husband, Rev. Frederick W. Haverkamp, to establish Westminster Presbyterian Church in Alexandria. Until the first church building opened in 1942, Mrs. Haverkamp was hosting congregants for services in their home on Virginia Avenue, packing in as many as 90 adults and children on Sunday mornings, and organizing church school classes.

And yet Mrs. Haverkamp also had a varied set of accomplishments that were all her own. As a student at Smith College around the turn of the century, she wrote a series of Shakespearean parodies, including "The Lamentable Tragedy of Omelet and Oatmealia," that were subsequently used in college English classes and provided royalty payments until shortly before her death in 1963 at age 84.

Her first husband was Congressman William P. Borland, a Democrat who represented Missouri from 1909 until 1919. While living in D.C., she caused a bit of a ruckus at a May 1912 meeting of the National Woman's Suffrage Association where members were hoping to form a congressional suffrage club. Ona Borland, who pointed out that both she and her husband supported equal suffrage, objected on the grounds that the group could not be called a congressional suffrage club because a majority of wives of congressmen were not present to approve the name. "Let the matter be put before the wives themselves, and let them, as is their right, determine whether or not the club be named congressional," she said, according to a *Washington Post* account. The motion was withdrawn, after which the article states that "the meeting was then declared adjourned, and tea was served."

In April 1915, the *Washington Post* also reported that a Standard electric car owned by Mrs. Borland was stolen from in front of their D.C. residence on 16th Street on a day that set a new record for stolen autos in D.C. Hers was the only one owned by a woman, however.

Mrs. Borland was widowed in 1919 when her husband succumbed to

Ona Haverkamp, wife of Frederick Haverkamp, the organizing minister of Westminster

pneumonia in France, where he was visiting American troops with other members of Congress. She returned to Missouri, where she worked for the Presbyterian Synod and met Haverkamp. During her time in Virginia, she was a national leader of the Woman's Christian Temperance Union, and she edited a monthly newspaper for the Virginia chapter for ten years.

> should fight for brotherhood, and decency, and better lives for all our people....
>
> It is from a strong and vital church—from the strength of all our churches—that government must draw its vision. In the teachings of our Saviour, there is no room for bigotry, for discrimination, for the embittered struggle of class against class, or for the hostilities of nation against nation.[67]

In those early decades, the church budget was tight and mainly consisted of personnel and building expenses. Cliff Johnson often mentioned in sermons the need for members to dig a little deeper in order to cover expenses. Church office staff turned over frequently, as did organists and music directors until Dana Brown was hired in 1957. (He served until 1990.)

As the church grew, it added associate pastors and a director of Christian Education. At least two other congregations attempted to lure Cliff Johnson from Westminster, so church leaders strove to provide competitive compensation packages. On the occasion of Johnson's 25th anniversary at Westminster, the congregation gave Cliff and his wife Allie a cash payment of $10,000 (equivalent to $84,000 in 2022 dollars) so that they could take a trip around the world, which they made in two stages in 1968 and 1969.

Benevolences—funds given by the church to support people in need outside of the church—made up a very small percentage of the budget in the 1940s and 1950s. Session records from 1947 indicate that Westminster contributed $7 to a Presbyterian denomination-wide fund for the "Negro Work" campaign. This campaign aimed to help organize new churches under Black leadership and to raise salaries for Black Presbyterian ministers. According to General Assembly minutes from 1947, "In view of the fact that the average salary of the Negro ministers is approximately $1,300, and in accord with the policy of the Assembly to raise salaries to an adequate level, we recommend that the Committee on Negro Work raise the salaries of Negro ministers as soon as possible, and that this year presbyteries and churches be encouraged to make additional gifts for this purpose."[68] (By comparison, Cliff Johnson earned $3,625 in 1948.)

---

67 Gerhard Peters and John T. Woolley, "Remarks in Alexandria, Va., at the Cornerstone Laying of the Westminster Presbyterian Church," The American Presidency Project, https://www.presidency.ucsb.edu/node/231167

68 Minutes of the Eighty-Seventh General Assembly of the Presbyterian Church in the United States, May 29-June 3, 1947, 105.

Westminster also participated in a 1953 General Assembly campaign to expand Stillman College, an HBCU in Tuscaloosa, Alabama, to a four-year liberal arts college, and to "improve church buildings and leadership in selected Negro communities," according to Session minutes.[69] The Session committed to a gift of $1,204 paid over three years, which represented about 10% of church's annual mission spending at that time. A letter was also sent to the congregation inviting them to make individual gifts to the campaign.

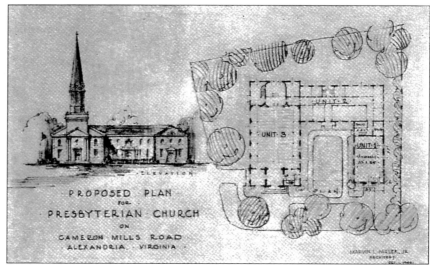

Architectural drawings for the new sanctuary

Nestled in a Segregated Neighborhood

In the wake of the 1954 Brown v. Board of Education decision, elected officials in Alexandria fully embraced the Byrd machine's "Massive Resistance." Nevertheless, according to author Douglas S. Reed, there was "significant local support for racial moderation."[70] The body of evidence from Cliff Johnson's sermons and from anecdotes buried in Session minutes from these years suggest that Westminster may have attracted some of these racial moderates into its membership. For example, in 1954, the Session passed a motion to employ a couple or single person, regardless of color, to act as caretaker for the church and allowing the caretaker the use of the church apartment. A Black man was hired as the building caretaker and lived in the apartment.[71]

The context in which this action took place is worth noting: The neighborhoods around Westminster and many other areas in Alexandria had restrictive covenants that prevented property from being "sold, transferred, leased, rented or conveyed to any person not of the Caucasian Race."[72] (In fact, the deed of sale for the parcel of land

---

69 Minutes of the Westminster Presbyterian Church Session, May 13, 1953.

70 Douglas S. Reed, *Building the Federal Schoolhouse: Localism and the American Educational State* (New York: Oxford University Press, 2014). Reed uses this phrase several times in his book.

71 Minutes of the Westminster Presbyterian Church Session, May 9, 1954.

72 Example of wording from the contract for the 1968 sale of a house on Tyler Place, just a few blocks from Westminster. There were also neighborhoods in Alexandria, such as Clover, which banned the sale of homes to Jews.

purchased by the Potomac Presbytery to establish Westminster very likely contained a similar covenant.[73]) The city of Alexandria was the last jurisdiction in the metropolitan area to enact an open housing law making these covenants illegal. Alexandria's version, which was passed in 1969 and took effect in 1970, contained a giant loophole: It exempted transactions that were made without a broker.[74] Although it cannot be confirmed, Cliff Johnson was likely one of the 56 Alexandria clergymen who signed a letter in 1967 calling upon Alexandrians to reject segregated housing practices.[75]

In 1961, according to Session minutes, "by formal action permission was granted for a colored pupil of the Minister of Music [Dana Brown] to use the organ of the church for practice."[76] In 1966, George Weber, a member of Shiloh Baptist Church, which was founded by former enslaved African-Americans in 1863, was invited to teach the youth group's Sunday School class.

Also around that same time, Johnson's son, Samuel, recalls a Black couple visiting the church for worship and shaking his father's hand at the door on their way out. After they left, an usher whispered to Associate Pastor Charlie Owens, "What do you think they were doing here?" Charlie calmly replied, "Worshiping God, I suppose."[77]

According to family lore, adds Samuel, prior to the very first Black visitors to the church, Johnson had announced from the pulpit that "if any Black person ever came to Westminster to worship, that person would be made completely welcome or he would immediately resign."[78]

1953

In 1953, the city of Alexandria began requiring all new street names that ran north and south to honor Confederate soldiers. This requirement was repealed only in 2014 after 66 streets had been named for Confederates. (For a list of those that still bear those names, see https://www.alexandriava.gov/buget-memos/fy-23-budget-qa-094how-many-streets-are-named-after-confederate-generals-soldiers-or.) Alexandria has more than twice as many objects named for Confederates than the city of Richmond, according to historian and author Ty Seidule.

---

73 "Examples of Deeds with Restrictive Covenants," handout from presentation by Dr. Krystyn Moon at Westminster, April 24, 2022.

74 Maurine McLaughlin, "Alexandria Moving on Open Housing," *Washington Post*, September 29, 1968, D2.

75 William R. MacKaye, "Alexandria Clergy Urge Open Housing," *Washington Post*, December 24, 1967, A1.

76 Minutes of the Westminster Presbyterian Church Session, April 12, 1961.

77 "Westminster at 60: Appreciating our Past...Celebrating Our Future," Westminster Presbyterian Church, 2000.

78 Email from Samuel Johnson, May 13, 2022.

A question from a member about how Westminster would respond if a Black person wished to join was taken up by the Session in 1962. According to the meeting minutes: "An open discussion was held for a short period pertaining to our policy on segregation. It was concluded that no formal action or restatement is necessary in view of the statement in our Book of Church Order and our own previous statements and actions, all of which provide for no distinctions as to race as it pertains to church membership and worship."[79]

Despite this affirmation, very few Black families have joined Westminster over the years. There were two Black families who were members during the 1970s,[80] and similar numbers in the 1980s and 1990s. Westminster has slightly increased its percentage of members of color in the past decade.

Church Leaders and Members React and Respond

In the weeks prior to the August 28, 1963, March on Washington for Jobs and Freedom, some Westminster members wished to host out-of-town participants at the church and in their homes. Westminster opted against having marchers stay on-site but a number of members offered up their homes. Even though the General Assembly refused to endorse the march, six local Presbyterian pastors participated (none from Westminster).[81]

During the tumultuous late 1960s, there were only a few noteworthy Session actions. At a called Session meeting held after worship on March 14, 1965, the Session voted to place envelopes in the pews for voluntary contributions to the family of Rev. James Reeb, who was killed by white supremacists on March 11 while marching from Selma to Montgomery.[82] Reeb was ordained as a Presbyterian minister and serving as a Unitarian Universalist minister when he was severely beaten and died a few days later from head injuries. (Three men were tried for Reeb's murder but were acquitted by an all-white jury.)

---

79 Minutes of the Westminster Presbyterian Church Session, May 2, 1962.

80 Church Information Form prepared by the 1980 Pastor Nominating Committee, Westminster Presbyterian Church.

81 "Forbidden by their General Assembly's action to carry any official placard using the Church's official 'P.C.U.S.' name, the group pushed the prohibition to the limit by making one that read 'Presbyterians U.S.,'" according to Thompson.

82 According to Thompson, the Potomac Presbytery sent money to repair the "terrorist-inflicted damage" that the Brown Chapel AME Church in Selma incurred.

Westminster's Men of the Church took up the topic of civil disobedience at their meeting in February 1968, with Associate Pastor John Watkins speaking about the "controversial action taken by our official governing bodies in the Presbyterian Church."[83] Watkins was referring to a statement from the General Assembly calling on churches to "give the support of Christian compassion to any member who, following his conscience in obedience to the Word, engages in civil disobedience."[84] Cliff Johnson addressed the statement in his sermon the Sunday following the Men of the Church gathering.

> As most of you know, the General Assembly of our denomination adopted a statement several years ago and has reaffirmed its position on at least one occasion that where there is an unjust law and where every other recourse has been exhausted there are times when, as a last measure, civil disobedience is to be accepted as a necessary measure.
>
> After much reflection I have come to the conclusion that I am opposed to the statement and would like to think that if I had been at the Assembly I would have voted against it… First, I think its intent is misunderstood by about 99% of the people who deal with it, both in and out of the church. Therefore I think its wording is unfortunate, misleading and self-defeating. The reaction of the men of this church the other night bears out what I am saying. The <u>intent</u> of the statement is no different from what has always been the position of the church and one with which practically every person here would agree—and that is this—that in a circumstance where a Christian has to choose between his loyalty to the state and his loyalty to Christ, he really has no choice, no matter what the personal cost may be. But you see that's not what is understood at all.
>
> The second reason I am opposed to the statement is that it does not deal at all with the issue that the Assembly was really trying to face. The Assembly was really trying to come to grips with racial injustice and how Christians should deal

---

83 Memorandum from Hugh Q. Alexander, "Activities of Men of Church in 1968," February 12, 1969.

84 "1965 Statement," https://index.pcusa.org/nxt/gateway.dll/SPCompilation%2F1489%2F1560%2F1564

> with it, but it doesn't say so anywhere in the statement.[85]

Civil disobedience may have been the impetus for the Session to create a subcommittee on community relations in late 1968. At the same time, it created a subcommittee on community concern, "to study any and all social needs of the community."[86]

It was perhaps under the auspices of this latter subcommittee that the Howard University Gospel Choir benefit concert was organized in partnership with Third Baptist Church in March 1970. The printed program for the concert, which was held just a few weeks after the death of Cliff Johnson and dedicated to his memory, described Johnson as someone who "strove for a better understanding between religious denominations and races" and noted that the event "was one of his last efforts for community betterment."

For the three decades before this concert, no sustained program of church mission giving directed to the local community appears to have existed. Most of the church's benevolence giving during this earlier period was forwarded to the denomination to support missionaries and Presbyterian colleges, and for special collections such as the Joy Offering, which provides assistance to current and retired church workers, and the Presbyterian Women's Birthday Offering.

That situation evolved in the late 1960s when the two Session subcommittees referenced above were created and in 1969 when the Potomac Presbytery's Church & Society committee made a set of recommendations to member churches. Among those recommendations:

- Encouraging churches to use their facilities as collateral in arranging loans for low- and moderate-income housing development, and encouraging congregations and individuals to invest monies in the Housing Revolving Fund of the Housing Development Corporation;

- Giving priority "to the concern for a racially inclusive ministry in the establishment and location of new churches;"

- Developing programs to enable congregants "to understand and respond creatively to the urban crisis and the problems of race and poverty in our

---

85 Johnson, "On Being Uncomfortable."

86 Minutes of the Westminster Presbyterian Church Session, December 11, 1968.

Church members assemble food for "Resurrection City" in Washington, D.C. in 1968

metropolitan area…and to act upon changes that are needed in suburban communities to relieve the crises in the central cities;"

- Demonstrating its concern "for the furtherance of economic justice by asking all agencies, committees, congregations and individual members to purchase goods and services only from companies that practice fair employment policies, and to explore with their banks with respect to hiring and upgrading members of minority groups and lending money to members of minority groups for housing and economic development."

There's no indication that Westminster considered adopting these recommendations, and it appears that the congregation was searching for what it perceived to be the proper balance between financial support and active engagement.

In 1969 Associate Pastor Watkins led a group of about 30 members to assess Westminster's mission and to consider the question, "How does a suburban church with its affluence and potential leadership relate effectively to the community in which it exists?" For the discussion he prepared a background document, "Toward a New Perspective," that makes the case that, unlike the inward activism that characterized the Church in the first half of the 20th century (think men's and women's groups, bowling and softball leagues), "the (C)hurch must leave the 20th century with an activism that is theologically rooted with an outward thrust" if it is to witness to the coming of the Kingdom of God.[87]

The following broad proposals resulted from these discussions:

- "Act in concert with other churches and synagogues in the community to

---

87 John M. Watkins, "Toward a New Perspective," undated. Watkins is using the word "church" to refer to the body of Christians who comprise Christ's Church.

provide a positive social and spiritual ministry to neighborhoods in which there is demonstrated evidence of need;

- Through its official organizations, take forthright positions in promoting necessary social change;

- Encourage and support individual members of the congregation and groups within the church in their efforts to involve themselves in effective Christian witness;

- Seek opportunities to implement policy positions adopted by the General Assembly;

- Provide for the education and training of its members so that they may understand the church's mission and contribute to its fulfillment;

- Allocate its resources—funds, physical facilities, and talents—to assure a continuing level of support for the accomplishment of objectives derived from the foregoing."[88]

From these lofty intentions at least one specific initiative developed: Northeast Ecumenical Parish, or NEEP, a group of six churches along the upper Russell Road corridor aiming to serve the Arlandria-Lynhaven area of Alexandria. Concerned about "the vast chasm of human need in the rapidly changing area and its inability to minister effectively to that need," NEEP aspired to establish a community center that would serve as a hub for various community services and agencies.[89] While there was an effort to hire a full-time director, NEEP as an organization appears to have been short-lived.

In the summer of 1970, the Westminster Session defeated a motion—by one vote—that would have permitted the use of the church facility for a day care center for Black families with limited means. The proposal had the support of the Program Committee, chaired by Elder Homer Walkup, and Associate Pastor Watkins, who was serving as interim senior pastor during these months following Johnson's death.[90] At the same meeting, the Session also *defeated* the following motion:

---

88 "Mission of the Church," attachment to "Toward a New Perspective," undated.

89 "A Prospectus for an Experimental Ministry for Northeast Alexandria," undated.

Rev. John Watkins was Associate Pastor from 1965 to 1971.

Resolved by the Session that Westminster reaffirm its commitment to the Third Baptist Church of Alexandria and to other groups to work for the betterment of the people in the Negro ghetto community, or areas, and to expand its benevolence programs to include support in the area of day care centers and similar activities.[91]

The opposition to the day care center may have been in part racially-motivated, but might also have reflected a sentiment on the part of the all-male Session that mothers should be at home caring for their children.[92] It also likely stemmed from the preference of some Westminster members for a more detached level of community involvement.

In his sermon the Sunday immediately following this Session meeting, Watkins's disappointment about the decision was palpable.

> This has been one of the most difficult weeks in my ministry to try to decide on a sermon… I want to share with you my theological pilgrimage of the last week. Now to lay down the ground rules, I'm not doing this in order to reopen a discussion about a decision that has been made. I do not wish to do that. Nor are my reflections an attempt in any sense to chastise those who disagree with my particular view or to convince you of my point of view. I simply want to state my point of view and you may take it or leave it as you wish. And neither in talking about my theological pilgrimage of the last week do I want to cast any aspersions on the Session. As I said earlier, in my judgment, they conducted themselves in a magnificent way, a way that truly allows them the honor of the title Elder, Ruling Elder, of this congregation. Neither do I want to convey in any sense any bitterness or disappointment or hatred. But rather I simply want to lay myself bare before

---

90 Minutes of the Westminster Presbyterian Church Session, July 15, 1970.

91 Ibid.

92 Later that same year, Catherine Longfellow became the first woman elected to the Westminster Session.

you because confession is good for the soul and I feel I will not rest until I have spoken as you have spoken to me. And I want to share my pastoral concern and love for this congregation with you.

There have been three passages that have haunted me for this past week, and for the past several weeks, and the first of these is found in the Gospel of Matthew in the 25th chapter beginning at the 44th verse: 'And then they also will answer, "Lord, when did we see thee hungry or thirsty or a stranger or naked or sick or in prison and did not minister to thee?" And then he, the Lord, will answer them, "Truly I say to you, as you did it not to one of the least of these, you did it not to me."'

As I have thought about this day care proposal that has occupied so much of our thoughts in the past week, and my thoughts for the past couple of months, I can never escape this passage. Never. And I try. When the negative comments came, when those who had good reasons why this should not happen, I wanted to back off. I wanted to go to the Session and say, 'Let's not even discuss it, let's just drop it.' For I am not a man who enjoys controversy, I'm not a man who enjoys a good fight, and I wanted to back off. But whenever that thought of backing off came into my mind, all I could see was Peter in the courtyard when the maid asked him whether he knew this man from Nazareth, Jesus, and Peter's answer was, 'Woman, I do not know him.'

I could not escape the idea and the concept that Christ was looking at me to see whether I, too, was going to deny him when the chips were down. If these mothers and children of whom we were talking are not one of the least of the brethren, then I simply do not know who the least are. I really don't. If these are not the least, who are they? Somebody in far off Africa? Somebody in Japan or Taiwan? Who are the least? And I don't know unless they are these mothers and children who have so little and simply want to get ahead.

Lord, when did we see thee hungry or thirsty or a stranger or naked or sick or in prison and did not minister to thee? As you did it not to one of the least of these, you did it not to me. I have never been able to get that passage out of my mind for it convicts me. [Long pause.]

Now there's another passage that bothered me, bothered me in the wee small hours of the morning when I lay in bed thinking about these things. And this is the passage found in Mark in the eighth chapter. It occurs right after Peter had tried to get Jesus to stop going to Jerusalem in order that he might not die. 'And Jesus in reply to Peter called to him the multitude with his disciples and said to them, "If any man would come after me, let him deny himself and take up his cross and follow me, for whoever would save his life will lose it and whoever loses his life for my sake and the Gospels will save it. For what does it profit a man to gain the whole world and forfeit his life?"'

This passage haunted me when I thought about all of the sacrifices that would be demanded of us in order to have a day care center here at Westminster. But somehow it always ended up that it was bricks and mortar and convenience that were being equated with people. And I myself could never make the equation work out. It was like trying to add apples and oranges and I simply couldn't do it. Yes, the center would have disrupted my days, again, probably more than anyone else's, and my schedule. And really as I thought about having a day care center here at Westminster, I really wondered at this particular time whether or not I could take any more disruptions to my day for there are enough of them now. But then Christ's life was disrupted by a cross so what were my petty sacrifices? Nothing, nothing at all.

HISTORIC MOMENT

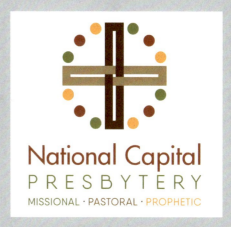

The Westminster sanctuary was the setting for history-in-the-making on January 6, 1972, when 1,000 people gathered for a service of reunification of the Washington City Presbytery (part of the United Presbyterians) and the Potomac Presbytery (part of the Southern Presbyterians) into the National Capital Union Presbytery (later renamed National Capital Presbytery). After 111 years of division caused by the Civil War, it would be another 11 years before the two denominations were joined nationally.

1968

In a sermon given on October 13, 1968, Dr. Cliff Johnson commented on the significance of WPC's geographical location.

> Here on the principal street of this residential area we have the firehouse, the church and the public school lined up one after the other—the firehouse representing the community's physical well-being, the school present for the community's intellectual well-being—and in between the Church responsible for the community's spiritual well-being.

Now some rightly pointed out that the building would not be used for a specific Christian purpose. That is, the school would not have as its primary goal Christian education. But then it occurred to me, we house the Republicans, the Harmonizers, the Scouts, the Braillers, square-dancing, all of whom may or may not ever mention Christ, I don't know. But all serve the community and they serve the community well. I, too, have been concerned to save the integrity of Westminster as an institution and as a church. I, too, was concerned that the building be put to a proper use. And in the equation, I have never felt that the building standing vacant was a proper use. I guess that my greatest fear was that in trying to save Westminster's integrity, we might be losing it.

'For whoever would save his life will lose it and whoever loses his life for my sake and the Gospels will save it. For what does it profit a man to gain the whole world and forfeit his life?' This passage would not let me go....

The decision has been made. So be it. Amen and amen. And now we must all live with it together. Let not the ones whose point of view prevailed be proud or haughty. But let them all confront their brethren with love and meekness and lowliness. And let not those whose point of view was lost be bitter and filled with any kind of hatred. Let no one allow self-righteousness to take hold but let us forebear one another in love.

Over and over again I've heard that this issue will split the congregation and I said to those who said that to me, I do not believe it. I do not believe it because we are bound

> together by Jesus Christ and none other. And being bound in Christ there is no room for pride, for we are all saved by grace. And there is no room for bitterness, or dissension, or hatred, for Christ, the one perfect man, was crucified wrongly and he prayed from the cross, 'Forgive them, father, for they know not what they do.' And if Christ can pray that prayer, then certainly we can forgive our brethren for whatever they have done or not done. Let us live together as those who know that in Christ there is one body, not many but one, one body, one spirit, one hope, one Lord, one faith, one baptism, one God and Father of us all.[93]

According to Pam Walkup, Homer's daughter, this disappointment eventually led to the creation of the Westminster Weekday Preschool in 1974, and from the beginning, there were a few scholarship slots for underprivileged children. Her father served on the Preschool Board for many years.

Community Collaborations

In a number of other local initiatives Westminster played a prominent role. Camp Glenkirk, which was the primary Presbyterian camp and conference center in the area for four decades beginning in 1960, held its first-ever Inner-City Camp in the summer of 1967. As William Thompson, who has documented the history of the National Capital Presbytery, colorfully describes, "It was largely a paternalistic effort since the volunteer camp counselors were all white, but the presence there of some of the Presbytery's 'heavyweight' Old Guard pastors—Graham Lacy, Cliff Johnson, Carl Pritchett—lent considerable credence to the effort and allayed the criticism that such ground-breaking efforts were only the concerns of the (dangerous) 'young Turks' of the Presbytery."[94]

In 1968, the Potomac Presbytery and the Washington City Presbytery joined forces on an experimental ministry known as the Landmark Shopping Center Ministries, created as "a partial reply to [the Potomac Presbytery's] continuing racial agenda issues," according to Thompson.[95] This novel ministry was designed to attract suburban apartment dwellers, who were perhaps seeking less traditional church programs, with such amenities as childcare, counseling, consumer information, art classes

---

93 Rev. John M. Watkins, "A Misunderstood Word," sermon delivered at Westminster Presbyterian Church in Alexandria, Va., on July 19, 1970, transcribed from audio recording.

94 Thompson, 310-311.

95 Thompson, 300.

and theater productions.[96] "[Johnson] was basically a traditionalist but he gamely supported this experimental ministry in his role as chairman of Potomac Presbytery's oversight committee," explains Thompson, and "one incident is illustrative of some of its problematical ways and why Dr. Johnson, who had rarely known a 'non-success,' finally surrendered his involvement with the Landmark ministry." As Thompson tells it, at one major "celebrative" Communion service, attendees were charged an entry fee, and he was standing next to Johnson when the Westminster pastor exclaimed, "I'll be damned if I am ever going to pay to attend a Communion service that celebrates the free grace of Jesus Christ!"[97] He turned on his heel and left. Landmark Ministries closed in 1970 and left the two Presbyteries with a loss of $1.3 million (equivalent to $9 million in 2022 dollars).[98]

A much more successful and long-lived collaboration began in 1969 when Westminster and a dozen other Alexandria churches formed ALIVE (Alexandrians Involved Ecumenically). ALIVE is the oldest and largest organization fighting poverty and hunger in the city, and Westminster has provided continued financial support without interruption for the 50-plus years of its existence.

Though the Session voted against participating in a General Assembly offering for "Negro" churches in 1971,[99] Westminster in the early years of Campbell's pastorate was stepping up its commitment to several other newly formed local organizations. Those included FISH (emergency services such as childcare, transportation, shopping, meals, etc.), FOLD (homes for teenage children who needed group foster care), Meals on Wheels, Hopkins House (services to the inner city of Alexandria, including Thanksgiving turkey distribution), Bridge (help to international students and others of foreign birth provided by the Presbytery and five churches in the Presbytery), and Guest House, which helps women successfully reenter the community from incarceration. The pattern of having a church member assigned as a representative to each of these organizations began during this time.

Campbell preached from an outline rather than a prepared text, so copies of his sermons are not available. But his widow, Winki, confirms that her husband's views on

---

96 Thompson, 301.

97 Thompson, 322.

98 Betty Medsger, "Presbytery Closes Shopping Center Mission," *Washington Post*, June 29, 1970, C1.

99 Minutes of the Westminster Presbyterian Church Session, September 15, 1971.

civil rights were similar to Johnson's and that her husband was more outspoken than some of his peers on matters of race. "Back in those days some Presbyterian ministers could lose their pulpit if they were supporting integration," says Winki, echoing comments that Cliff Johnson made about the "freedom of the pulpit" that Westminster afforded him. "But he was also old enough to know that you can't get too far ahead of congregation" on divisive issues.[100]

Sarah Yancey, who was a member of Westminster in the 1960s and 1970s and was close to the Campbells, recalls that "Don was very much an advocate for racial equality," though he didn't necessarily use the pulpit to advance the cause.[101] Campbell, who worked to unify the southern Potomac Presbytery and the northern Washington City Presbytery in 1972 (see "Historic Moment," page 51), died prematurely at age 51 of a heart attack while vacationing at Chautauqua in the summer of 1979.

"Have I Made a Mistake?"

On Dr. George Pera's first evening in Alexandria after having accepted the senior pastor position at Westminster, a group of members took him on a driving tour of the city, including the statue of the Confederate soldier that stood at the time at Washington and Prince Streets.[102] Pera remembers wondering, "Have I made a mistake? I tossed and turned that night. I came from a very different background from some of the other Westminster pastors."

The church where Pera landed in 1980 was, as he describes, "southern," and most of the members had witnessed segregation at some time. "This guy from the north shouldn't lecture them too much on their experience," says Pera, in describing the sense of some in the congregation. He felt that his role was to open up the dialogue. "I didn't want to do anything that would shut down the conversation. You can blast them from the pulpit and turn people off but that wasn't my style."[103]

Nevertheless, in 2014 when Pera was named a Living Legend of Alexandria, he was

---

100 Conversation with Winki Campbell, February 28, 2022.

101 Conversation with Sarah Yancey, January 13, 2022. Sarah Yancey served as campaign manager for Connie Ring's first successful city council campaign. She and Connie were both members of the Pastor Nominating Committee that called Dr. George Pera.

102 The statue was removed in June 2020 following the murder of George Floyd in Minneapolis by white police officer Derek Chauvin.

Dr. George Pera was Senior Pastor from 1980 to 1995.

quoted as saying, "[My] interest in the world about me has served me well in my preaching. The theologian Reinhold Niebuhr said when a pastor writes a sermon, he should hold the Bible in one hand and a newspaper in the other."[104] Pera is certain that he never preached a sermon specifically on the topic of race relations but that his viewpoints would come through nonetheless. "I could not have avoided the topic—that's not my nature—but I really worked behind the scenes with leaders of the Black community and did my own part when I could."

The Rev. Dr. Elbert Ransom Jr. attended Westminster for a couple of years in the 1980s. Ransom was a cousin of Medgar Evers and a Black Baptist preacher who had served as an assistant to MLK in Montgomery, Ala. and marched with him. He preached a couple of times from the Westminster pulpit and, having been trained as an operatic singer, sang solos accompanied by music director Dana Brown. He later became an associate pastor at Alfred Street Baptist Church and a faculty member at Virginia Theological Seminary.[105] Ransom describes the Westminster congregation as "inviting, friendly, and paying a lot of attention to me," and that "the cream of the crop went to Westminster, the people who were doing big things in Alexandria."[106] But he does not recall that the church was particularly involved in local outreach or social justice.

Ransom and Pera became close friends and he helped open doors for Pera to the Black community. Along with Rabbi Jack Moline of Agudas Achim Congregation, they worked to bring together local leaders of faith traditions and denominations. In time,

---

103 Conversation with Dr. George Pera, February 1, 2022.

104 https://alexandrialegends.org/rev-george-pera/

105 For more about Ransom's career and accomplishments, see https://alexandrialegends.org/bert-ransom-creates-a-chorus-of-hope/

106 Conversation with Rev. Dr. Elbert Ransom, March 17, 2022.

Black leaders in Alexandria would seek Pera's input on local issues. Pera and former city manager Vola Lawson served as honorary co-chairs for the mayoral campaign of William Euille, who became Alexandria's first Black mayor.

In the mid-1980s, Pera and the long-time senior pastor of Alfred Street Baptist Church, Rev. John Peterson, established a discussion group between members of the two congregations. Candace Rush, who along with her late husband Henri participated in these gatherings, recalls that "we went into this with the hope that regular discourse between our churches would bring about a more comfortable level of conversation."[107] Over the course of about two years, two dozen people would meet monthly to discuss different topics. One of the underlying questions for Westminster members was the dilemma posed by MLK: Why is 11:00 a.m. on Sunday morning the most segregated hour in America? "So often there were just cultural differences" that came to light in the way the two congregations chose to worship, says Rush. "The length of the service [at Black churches] is an issue for whites."

Pera says he never witnessed overt racism from any members during his tenure. "They would have heard back from me in two seconds!" And he actively called out racism when he saw it in the community, such as a hateful conversation that he overheard among police officers outside of the Everly-Wheatley funeral home and promptly reported to the chief of police.

In another incident, Pera directly confronted police racism. An elderly Westminster member had a Black male nursing assistant who worked an overnight shift in her home near Quaker Lane. Each night while driving to his client's home, he would be stopped by police who would interrogate him about why he was in the neighborhood. The church member relayed this situation to Pera, who arranged with the nursing assistant for Pera and another church member to ride in the backseat of the aide's car one night on the way to the client's home. When they were stopped by police on Quaker Lane, Pera took the officers' picture and told them that he was sending it to the *Alexandria Gazette*. "The cops stopped harassing him, but [George's wife] Nancy and I received a number of threatening phone calls."

As pastor, Pera volunteered with the local organizations, such as ALIVE and Senior Services of Alexandria, that the church was supporting financially. (Pera eventually

---

107 Conversation with Candace Rush, February 28, 2022.

Students at the United Orphanage and Academy in Moi's Bridge, Kenya

served on the Senior Services board for 20 years, including two as board president.) In 2014, Pera said in an interview, "When you want to get people involved, you just can't stand there and point to what needs doing. You have to take the paint brush, climb the ladder and start painting. That's how you get people involved. You lead by doing."[108]

The connections that Henri and Candace Rush developed in Zaire and Kenya during visits there in the 1980s and 1990s would lay the groundwork for one of Westminster's most enduring legacies and provide the motivation for an unprecedented commitment of mission spending by the congregation: United Orphanage and Academy in Moi's Bridge, Kenya. The orphanage was founded in 2001, under the Westminster leadership of Rev. Stuart Broberg, to provide a peaceful and safe home for children from various ethnic groups who were in conflict with one another. Westminster has funded the construction of dormitories, toilet facilities, a dining hall, kitchen, office and storage space; dug a well; provided for facility upgrades to enable connection to

---

[108] https://alexandrialegends.org/rev-george-pera/

the electric grid; and purchased a 14-passenger van, all with budgeted funds combined with contributions from individual members of the congregation and other churches.

Total enrollment at the Academy is almost 150 students, including approximately 40 scholarship students from the surrounding area whose educations are made possible with funding from Westminster and other churches in the U.S. Of the 150 students, about 55 (ranging in age from four to 18) live at the orphanage, and another six attend college elsewhere. Westminster resources also provide support for those children who continue past secondary school to college or technical school.

In 2011, Westminster instituted the Westminster Community Grant program to support local organizations serving the needs of our local community in the areas of children, hunger, education, shelter, and self-sufficiency. These grants, which are in addition to annual congregational support to a number of worthy charities, allow organizations to respond quickly to special needs that can't be covered by their regular operating budgets. By the end of 2022, more than $250,000 had been distributed to dozens of organizations.[109]

Pandemic, Racial Reckoning and Personal Tragedy

When Rev. Whitney Fauntleroy was called to Westminster from North Carolina in 2017 as Associate Pastor for Youth and Young Adults, she was the first person of color to serve on the pastoral staff at Westminster. (Rev. Evangeline Taylor became the second in 2018.) Fauntleroy's connection with the youth and their families, and her poetically powerful and honest preaching style were quickly admired and embraced by the congregation and staff.

Like Johnson a half century earlier, Fauntleroy challenged the congregation to reject our society's racial status quo—a status quo that has painfully morphed over the decades into systems that continue to perpetuate inequality in many facets of life for people of color. In 2020, in the midst of a pandemic lock-down that profoundly affected her ministry to the church's youth, and amid heightened national awareness of racial issues after the murder of George Floyd, Fauntleroy was asked by the youth and their families to preach on July 5, a Sunday when another pastor had been scheduled to preach.

---

[109] Go to https://wpc-alex.org/westminster-community-grant for a list of all past recipients.

2006

Rev. Dr. Larry Hayward became Westminster's fifth called senior pastor in 2004. This excerpt is from "Lincoln, King and Scripture," written by Hayward and published in *Ripon Forum* magazine, April/May 2006.

" …Lincoln and King used Biblical language that spoke to community. Their language transcended differences, religious and otherwise. At the deepest, most personal level, Lincoln and King affirmed that the opportunity for individuals to live freely and flourish is a—if not the—fundamental promise and premise of American life. These two speeches [Lincoln's Second Inaugural Address and King's 'I Have a Dream' speech] of these two leaders are certainly among the most historically significant uses of scripture in American history….

The capacity to give voice to individualism is crucial to Americans. But at our best, we recognize that for individualism to flourish, communities must be healthy.

Lincoln and King captured this creative balance in their use of scripture. For our nation to flourish, we must capture the balance between individualism and community. For our nation to flourish 'under God,' we would benefit by looking at the way Lincoln and King used scripture. "

> I did not want to be here… I am here because of the youth. The high school youth of this church have inspired me in ways and days when joy is hard to find. A few of our youth told me they wanted to hear from me. I didn't want to speak. And then a parent of three, two of them youth, explained to me why they thought the church needed to hear from me. I didn't want to speak. But then I thought about the people I've grown to love during the sleepless nights on church floors, both upstairs and abroad. And I decided to speak. So here I am, and here we are.…
>
> I didn't want to be here today but there are some youth who I have been in conversation with who asked important questions and seek even better answers. I'm here because they are here and they are in the streets crying for justice wanting us to be better. I am here because of the youth of Westminster, and I am here because of the youth of University United Methodist Church in Chapel Hill, North Carolina, a church just a stone's throw away from the place where the statue of Silent Sam once stood tall. And when I was blessed to walk alongside those youth, I did not have the courage to stand in my melanin-soaked God-given gifts and speak about the pain of racism when I had their hearts, their minds, and their ears. I wanted to talk to them desperately when my soul ached after the verdict in the killing of Trayvon Martin and the subsequent case. I wanted to teach them how to lament with those who suffer because their bodies are Black, but I was scared. I no longer am scared. I owe it to those youth, to these youth and the bruised bodies of my ancestors to not be scared and to speak up. It is no doubt one of the greatest honors of my time here to be able to lead worship with not the future but the now, the youth who asked me, could they lead worship, and so I share the mic even when I have so much to say. I share it not with the future but with the now because we are here, they are here. I am here.[110]

On this Independence Day weekend, Whitney chose to preach and teach on this passage from Paul's letter to the Romans: "I know that good doesn't live in me—that is, in my body. The desire to do good is inside of me, but I can't do it. I don't do the good that

I want to do, but I do the evil that I don't want to do. But if I do the very thing that I don't want to do, then I'm not the one doing it anymore. Instead, it is sin that lives in me that is doing it."[111]

> I would imagine that you have read the words 'systemic or structural racism,' or 'white privilege,' or something similar, <u>a lot</u> over the last few weeks. Maybe those words and concepts made you feel uncomfortable…uh, I hope they do. Scaffolds of sin, be they the Constitution, or a college, or a corporation, should make us squirm. Get used to what makes you feel uncomfortable during this peculiarly painful American summer.
>
> I saw this poem by [Nayyirah] Waheed that I want to share: 'I think one of the most pathological things I've ever seen is stabbing someone and telling them their pain over being stabbed is making you sad. Signed, White Guilt.' With what seems like white America's wholesale awakening to sins of this soil from the New York islands to the Gulf Stream waters bubbling up in CNN scrolls, think pieces and syllabi getting passed around on the internet, some of you may be asking, 'What can I do, what can we—that's you—as white people, do?' Good question. Keep asking it. Keep being uncomfortable and finding things that make you squirm enough, squirm enough to be angry to want better. You can want to do better, and you can even believe you are doing better. You are watching your language, or reading books, amplifying new and different voices, maybe even sitting with all of this in a new way that tears at your very soul. But all of that, while valuable, in a sense, is also of no value. We can't help but do what we don't want to do. Nobody's perfect.
>
> I find the apostle Paul and his writings difficult for a variety of reasons, namely that Paul is a person of extremes. There is only black and white, there is never any gray. He violently persecuted Christians and then goes on a world apology

---

110 Rev. Whitney K. Fauntleroy, "Nobody's Perfect," sermon delivered at Westminster Presbyterian Church in Alexandria, Va., July 5, 2020, transcribed from audio recording accessed at https://wpcalex.sermon.net/main/main/21621840.

111 Romans 7:18-20, Common English Bible.

and apologetics tour to save souls. Paul, our problematic persecutor-turned-preacher going through Asia Minor saying wild stuff about women and slaves and circumcision and contradicting himself all along the way. However, today in these verses in Romans, I have a little—shocker, gulp—sympathy for Paul. Paul admits that he is trash, even as he went from the extremes of violently persecuting Christians to falling in love with Jesus and fervently sharing the Gospel, he is captive to sin. Even when Paul's ultimate desire is to enjoy God always, he fails. We fail. I can't help but do what I don't want to do. Paul can't help but do what he doesn't want to do. We can't help but do what we don't want to do. Nobody's perfect. We are born sinners. Um, news flash: It is really, really, hard to be a Christian. Get out while you can.

Rev. Whitney Fauntleroy was Associate Pastor from 2017 to 2022.

This weekend as we celebrate this country's first steps into independence, what is true freedom? I'm not talking about freedom earned from victories in battle or elevated language, rhetoric, and ideals of government documents. I'm talking about the ultimate freedom for those of us who try as hard as it may be to follow Christ. What is freedom in Christ and what does it cost? The good news that Paul reminds us of in these words in Romans is that when we get to the very heart of our humanity, we cannot help but be humbled by God's divinity. Our being human, though depraved, desolate and dejected as we may be, and can't seem to not be, only means that God in the person of Jesus Christ, knows this depravity, desolation and dejection, when he called out for his mother as he died at the hands of the state, when he couldn't breathe as the temple was torn, when blood and water flowed from his side as he hung limp on that lynching tree we call the cross. That Jesus Christ knows all too well what it is to be human, to suffer, but also in him, in Christ, the sight of Calvary's mountain became not the haunted story of his end or ours, but the beginning of resurrected hope of the miracle of God's divinity to scream out 'Victory is mine, victory is mine, I told Satan get thee behind, victory is mine today.'

In the cries of that baby in the scent of the hay in Bethlehem, and the cries of God on the cross, we can proclaim this ridiculous hope of resurrection that freedom is coming, freedom is coming, freedom is coming, yes, I know. Our humanity proves the need for God—God's grace, God's spirit, God's peace. Freedom is not only in the wondrous cross, but in the wonders of creation that God in her wisdom called good and called us into her bosom promising not to let us go even when we have strayed. Freedom is in Golgotha, yes, but is also in the morning fish fry by the shore with loved ones during resurrected mornings. Freedom is not just the bloody Savior, but the one who calls us beloved. Freedom is not just in the wilderness of exile, but in the manna that falls daily. Freedom is in Jesus Christ, the wounded healer, who defeats the power that seems undefeatable, the power of sin.

And what does this freedom cost you? Well, it is not free. It is not a resignation that we can just be silent, and complicit to the forces of sin, but that we seek the kingdom of God and God's righteousness even when we don't want to. And even when we know we aren't able to and even when we fail miserably. Freedom costs us the chipping away at systems and structures. It costs us trying when it doesn't make sense. It costs us the price of looking foolish—foolish enough to act like the work of Jesus means something not just for you, but for me, not just for the church or even just for Christians, but for the world. Freedom costs your feet that march to the beat of the kingdom dance parties, feet that don't become beautiful because they are never touched but because they have trampled in the dirt of depravity only to have been made beautiful by the calluses of what can seem like the futility of working for a future not yet here. Freedom costs us dying daily and picking up heavy crosses even as we lay our burdens down. Freedom costs us a mighty sacrifice, even when we might not live to see our return on investment.

> Freedom in Christ is a mighty conundrum, but it is here for you, for Paul, for me, for us. I cannot help but do what I do not want to do. Nobody's perfect but keep trying. Be perfect as your father in heaven is perfect.[112]

The year 2020 would turn out to be Fauntleroy's "annus horribilis." Earlier that year, Fauntleroy had received a grant from the Lilly Endowment in conjunction with the Foundations of Christian Leadership program at Duke Divinity School to involve Westminster youth in leading the congregation to think about racial and ethnic equity from a theological perspective. But those plans were thwarted in September when life-saving surgery to remove a tumor from the top of her spine left her paralyzed in both legs and partially paralyzed in one arm.

After long hospital stays and thousands of hours of physical therapy, through sheer determination and perseverance and perhaps divine intervention, she progressed from wheelchair to walker to cane to walking unassisted. The Westminster community responded with meals, companionship, transportation, financial assistance, prayers and love. Even though she was on medical leave through the end of 2022, she continued to minister to her flock and beyond.

In late 2022, Fauntleroy asked the Westminster congregation to dissolve her pastoral relationship with the church, and she preached a final sermon there on January 8, 2023. Fauntleroy continues to serve in ministry around the National Capital Presbytery.

---

112 Fauntleroy, "Nobody's Perfect."

In March 2022, Rev. Dr. Larry Hayward and Rev. Maggie Hayward led a group of Westminster and Northwood Presbyterian (Silver Spring, Maryland) members on a pilgrimage to important sites of the civil rights movement in Alabama.

CONCLUSION

Whether it's a stirring message delivered from the pulpit by a young white pastor during the turbulent 1950s or by a young Black pastor following the murder of George Floyd; a compromise crafted with other city officials to extend equal opportunities to Black students; or examples of leadership that motivate others to act, Westminster Presbyterian Church and its congregation have—in some cases but not always—responded to the struggle for civil rights over the years.

The journey toward racial justice is far from over. There is much work to do—both as a congregation and as individual members. The content of the next chapter in that journey is taking shape now.

" There comes a time when one must take a position that is neither safe, nor politic, nor popular, but he must take it because conscience tells him it is right. "

*— Martin Luther King Jr.,
from "A Proper Sense of Priorities,"
speech delivered in Washington, D.C.
on February 6, 1968*

ACKNOWLEDGMENTS

As the member of the Therefore Project committee with the longest tenure at Westminster, I was the logical person to investigate and document the church's history as it relates to the civil rights movement. I began this work with low expectations of how much useful information that I would be able to unearth and with trepidation about how the church had conducted itself during the early and middle decades of the last century. What unfolded was a rich and fascinating journey that was enormously gratifying, and I feel privileged to have been the "somebody" whom Dr. Cliff Johnson in 1958 predicted "will go back and write what was done in this community in this conflict."

Along the way, I benefited greatly from many individuals who took time to answer questions, dig up information, share remembrances and check my facts. Those include: Jane Bourdow, Rosalind Bovey, Winki Campbell, Don Dahmann, Becky Davies, Ellen Hamilton, Cathy Hunter, Cliff Johnson Jr., Samuel Johnson, Jack Moline, Jan Moody (National Capital Presbytery), Dr. Krystyn Moon (the University of Mary Washington), Charlene Peacock (Presbyterian Historical Society), Dr. George Pera, Rev. Dr. Elbert Ransom, Jim Roberts, Candace Rush, Pam Walkup, Sarah Yancey, and the staff of the Local History/Special Collections department at the Barrett branch of Alexandria Library.

I'm deeply indebted to Connie, Jane and Rusty Ring for their contributions. Nancy Hall Berens, Donald Gordon, Rev. Dr. Larry Hayward, Anne Ledyard, Jim Muyskens and David Wilcox provided helpful comments on earlier drafts. The publishing of this book was supported by the Van de Water Scholarship Fund, in honor of Clara Beth Van de Water's service as Director of Adult Education at Westminster from 1982 to 2015.

And, lastly, a shout-out to all of the former and current Westminster members who over the years have maintained our church archives. Without their careful and unsung efforts, this book would not have been possible.

APPENDIX

Therefore Committee Report to the Westminster Presbyterian Church Session

In the wake of the George Floyd killing on May 25, 2020, and its aftermath, Westminster Presbyterian Church Session created the Therefore Committee to explore ways that our church could address the searing racial issues facing our country. The Committee met virtually 13 times over five months for 90 minutes per meeting.

To generate ideas about how the Church could respond, Committee members led 16 discussion groups involving 61 WPC members, one group involving 27 members of the Session, and two groups with seven members of the staff. Those discussions generated a number of ideas and suggestions that the Therefore Committee reviewed. The Committee ultimately boiled down those ideas to nine specific recommendations for the Session to consider.

Over the course of our discussions, it became evident that articulating some broader guiding principles for how WPC should respond to social and political issues would assist our deliberations. Those principles could also be useful for future Sessions in dealing with controversial societal events, and for use in classes to help members and officers learn about Westminster's approach to these events. So in addition to the specific recommendations, we offer those guiding principles for the Session to consider.

The Committee strongly recommends that addressing racial challenges be an ongoing effort at Westminster. We urge the Session to continue this Committee's charter for at least one more year for periodic discussions about the progress the Church is making, and for making further recommendations as warranted. Individual members of the Committee will also make themselves available as resources for staff and committees as they seek to interpret and implement these recommendations.

Therefore Committee Members

Larry Hayward, Pastor
Whit Ayres, Co-Chair
Anne Ledyard, Co-Chair
Mike Duodu
Donald Gordon
Molly Harper

Melissa LoPresti
Jill Maguire
Kristi Meyers
Jim Muyskens
Erskine Wells
Melynda Wilcox

Recommendations

1. Create and promote dialogues like the discussion with Representatives John Lewis and Fred Upton to explore racial issues.

2. Review and, if necessary, modify purchasing and contracting policies and practices to be sure that minority-owned businesses are able to compete for Church business.

3. Review personnel policy and procedures to ensure that hiring practices are inclusive, and support diversity, equity, and inclusion training for clergy, staff, and officers of the Church.

4. Create an inventory of our mission programs to evaluate the extent to which they promote racial understanding and equality, with an eye to exploring how we can expand our activities.

5. Sponsor and promote civil rights pilgrimages to key local and national sites in the history of the civil rights movement in America.

6. Create a collection of books and articles in the church library and website for members who wish to learn more about the history of racism, the many and diverse ideas about how to achieve racial understanding and equality.

7. Offer Christian Formation courses, workshops, and resources for adults, youth, children and their families that address multiple facets of racism and responses to racism.

8. Offer an Adult Formation course about the history of Westminster and the Presbyterian Church denomination regarding racial issues, and write a history of Westminster relative to race.

9. Utilize the Dessert and Dialogue program to include discussions around diversity, equity, and inclusion.

Guiding Principles When Dealing With Social and Political Issues

Westminster Presbyterian Church views its primary mission as ministering to its members and their families in the whole of their lives, spiritual, moral, social, political, and personal.

Given the proximity to our nation's capital, Westminster includes many members involved in political activities, and their views span the spectrum from very liberal to very conservative.

We seek to make everyone, regardless of political orientation, feel welcome, accepted, and affirmed as Christians as we engage with one another.

That means that our Church will be thoughtful about taking public stands that could be viewed as political positions, be they liberal or conservative.

That does not mean that Westminster will never take a position on issues of social or political import, but it will do so with substantial deliberation that seeks to understand and reflect a consensus of views among its members, particularly when the Session speaks beyond our membership to the larger community or world.

Timeline

May 25, 2020	George Floyd killed
June 23, 2020	Session approved discussion groups on how WPC should respond
July 5, 2020	Session adopted statement regarding the killing drafted by Ben Kennedy, Jim Muyskens, Curt Powell, and Tim Shaw
September 22, 2020	Session approved Therefore Committee Project proposed by Larry Hayward
December 2, 2020	Session approved Therefore Committee members nominated by Larry Hayward, Sue Aland, Mary Filicetti, and Tim Shaw
February–May, 2021	Discussion groups with WPC members and staff
June, 2021	Recommendations and Principles adopted and recommended to the Session

Origins of the Therefore Committee Project

This Committee grew out of the charge included in the Response to Racism statement adopted by the Session:

In the immediate days ahead, our community will define a plan to bring about more justice, equity, inclusion, safety, compassion, trust, and love. In the short-term, we will seek to strengthen our community by uplifting the disadvantaged and fearful and assist those in crises. We will not stop there, however. We commit to long-term empowerment and hope, so that we might one day effect true healing, absolution, and forgiveness. We will walk with any seeking constructive change and condemn those who would use violence to block progress.

The Committee's name comes from Paul's letter to the Romans:

*I appeal to you **therefore**, brothers and sisters, by the mercies of God, to present your bodies as a living sacrifice, holy and acceptable to God, which is your spiritual worship. ²Do not be conformed to this world, but be transformed by the renewing of your minds, so that you may discern what is the will of God—what is good and acceptable and perfect. (Romans 12:1-2)*

The Committee fully recognizes that our efforts are but an initial step for Westminster in confronting the longstanding effects of racism in our community and culture. We have made a good faith effort to take that initial step.

BIBLIOGRAPHY

"Alexandria Library Sit-In." https://en.wikipedia.org/wiki/Alexandria_Library_sit-in

"Alexandria's Schools and the Law." Editorial. *Washington Post*, May 9, 1973.

Battiata, Mary and Jura Koncius. "Beatley Defeats GOP's Calhoun in Alexandria." *Washington Post*, May 5, 1982.

"Beverley Charges 'Gestapo' Tactics in School Dispute." *Alexandria Gazette*, October 4, 1958.

"Borland Dies Abroad." *Washington Post*, February 22, 1919.

"Brown v. Board and the Desegregation of Alexandria City Public Schools." Alexandria City Public Schools, https://www.acps.k12.va.us/Page/2402

"Brown v Board: It Takes a Community to Make a Difference." Alexandria City Public Schools, February 18, 2019, https://www.acpsk12.org/news/?p=12322

"Brown v. Board: 60 Years On – The Action that Took 14 Years to Complete." Alexandria City Public Schools, February 2, 2019, http://www.acpsk12.org/news/?p=12150

"Clash on Suffrage: Wives of Lawmakers at Odds Over Organizing Club." *Washington Post*, May 15, 1912.

Dewar, Helen. "Va. Voter Residency Rule Hit." *Washington Post*, September 21, 1968.

Dole, Kenneth. "Sermons with Humor Draw Flock to Church." *Washington Post*, March 7, 1959.

Edwards, Paul G. "Alexandria Asked for Action on Desegregation of Schools." *Washington Post*, February 25, 1972.

Fauntleroy, Rev. Whitney K. "Nobody's Perfect." Westminster Presbyterian Church, July 5, 2020, transcribed from audio recording accessed at https://wpcalex.sermon.net/main/main/21621840.

"Four Autos Are Stolen: Thieves Make New Record for One Day in Getting Away with Cars." *Washington Post*, April 14, 1915.

Hayward, Rev. Dr. Larry R. "Lincoln, King and Scripture." *Ripon Forum*, April/May 2006.

Hodes, David. "Standing Up." *Northern Virginia Magazine*, August 21, 2014, https://northernvirginiamag.com/culture/culture-features/2014/08/21/standing-up/

Jenkins, Kent, Jr. "'Reactionary' Seeks a New Label: Mayor." *Washington Post*, April 28, 1988.

Johnson, Dr. Cliff. "Brotherhood Week." *Alexandria Gazette*, February 20, 1960.

Johnson, Dr. Cliff. *Every Moment an Easter.* Westminster Presbyterian Church, 1962.

Johnson, Dr. Cliff. *Jesus' Financial Troubles.* Westminster Presbyterian Church, undated.

Living Legends of Alexandria. https://alexandrialegends.org

Lyles, Mable T. *Caught Between Two Systems: Desegregating Alexandria's Schools 1954-1973* (2006)

MacKaye, William R. "Alexandria Clergy Urge Open Housing." *Washington Post*, December 24, 1967.

Marriott, Michel. "Alexandria Politics Shape School Board." *Washington Post*, July 13, 1983.

McElhatton, Jim. "A School Cook's Forgotten Civil Rights Stand." *Alexandria Times*, March 22, 2018, https://alextimes.com/2018/03/civilrightsstand/

McLaughlin, Maurine. "Alexandria Backs Open Housing." *Washington Post*, February 12, 1969.

McLaughlin, Maurine. "Alexandria Moving on Open Housing." *Washington Post*, September 29, 1968.

McLaughlin, Maurine. "The City Still Faces South a Century After Civil War." *Washington Post*, June 26, 1969.

Medsger, Betty. "Presbytery Closes Shopping Center Mission." *Washington Post*, June 29, 1970.

Moon, Dr. Krystyn. "Alexandria in 1969: Police Violence, Race Relations, and a Call for Reform." Office of Historic Alexandria.

Moon, Dr. Krystyn. "Examples of Deeds with Restrictive Covenants." Handout from presentation at Westminster Presbyterian Church, April 24, 2002.

"1965 Statement." Presbyterian Church in the United States. https://index.pcusa.org/nxt/gateway.dll/SPCompilation%2F1489%2F1560%2F1564

North Ridge Lore Revisited (North Ridge Citizens' Association, 2000).

Omang, Joanne. "Alexandria Adopts Pupil Mixing Plan." *Washington Post*, May 15, 1973.

Omang, Joanne. "Alexandria Board Narrows Choices on Pupil Changes." *Washington Post*, May 1, 1973.

Omang, Joanne. "Alexandria Busing Held Excessive." *Washington Post*, August 22, 1973.

Omang, Joanne. "'Moral Issue' Decides Busing Plan." *Washington Post*, May 16, 1973.

Omang, Joanne. "Schools Decision Deferred." *Washington Post*, May 10, 1973.

"On Our Way…Rejoicing! 1940 –1990." Westminster Presbyterian Church, September 1990.

"Ona Haverkamp, 84: Editor of WCTU Paper." *Washington Post*, August 4, 1963.

Peters, Gerhard and John T. Woolley. "Remarks in Alexandria, Va., at the Cornerstone Laying of the Westminster Presbyterian Church." The American Presidency Project, https://www.presidency.ucsb.edu/node/231167

Presbyterian Church in the United States. "Minutes of the Eighty-Seventh General Assembly." May 29 – June 3, 1947.

Reed, Dr. Douglas S., *Building the Federal Schoolhouse: Localism and the American Education State* (New York: Oxford University Press, 2014)

"Samuel Tucker: Unsung Hero of the Civil Rights Movement." City of Alexandria, https://www.alexandriava.gov/museums/samuel-tucker-unsung-hero-of-the-civil-rights-movement

"School Unit Gets First GOP Member." *Washington Post*, June 26, 1969.

Seidule, Ty. *Robert E. Lee and Me: A Southerner's Reckoning with the Myth of the Lost Cause* (New York: St. Martin's Press, 2021)

Smith, J. Y. "Maj. Gen. Harry Vaughn, Aide to President Truman, Dies at 87." *Washington Post*, May 22, 1981, https://www.washingtonpost.com/archive/local/1981/05/22/maj-gen-harry-vaughan-aide-to-president-truman-dies-at-8/e96a79b4-811a-4ca7-b8c3-560c622ec9e5/

Smith, Timothy R. "William E. Bason, Pastor of Alexandria Church." *Washington Post*, May 17, 2011, https://www.washingtonpost.com/local/obituaries/william-e-basom-pastor-of-alexandria-church/2011/05/14/AFVFX45G_story.html

Sullivan, Patricia. "Lawyer Samuel Tucker and his Historic 1939 Sit-in at Segregated Alexandria Library." *Washington Post*, August 7, 2014, https://www.washingtonpost.com/local/lawyer-samuel-tucker-and-his-historic-1939-sit-in-at-segregated-alexandria-library/2014/08/05/c9c1d38e-1be8-11e4-ae54-0cfe1f974f8a_story.html

Swain, Claudia. "Alexandria Library Sit-In, 1939." Boundary Stones, WETA's Local History Website, https://boundarystones.weta.org/2016/11/29/alexandria-library-sit-1939

"There Was a Man…." Editorial. *Alexandria Gazette*, February 11, 1970.

Thompson, William E. "'A Set of Rebellious Scoundrels': Three Centuries of Presbyterians Along the Potomac" (National Capital Presbytery, 1989)

Watkins, Rev. John M. "Toward a New Perspective." Undated manuscript.

Watkins, Rev. John M. "A Prospectus for an Experimental Ministry for Northeast Alexandria." Undated manuscript.

"Westminster at 60: Appreciating our Past…Celebrating Our Future." Westminster Presbyterian Church, 2000.

"Westminster Presbyterian Church: Sharing God's Word, Showing God's Love and Serving God's World." Westminster Presbyterian Church, April 2004.

Westminster Presbyterian Church Archives (session minutes from 1940 to 1980, memorandum from Dr. Cliff R. Johnson, memorandum from Men of the Church, printed sermons and audiotapes, letter from John Watkins, manuscripts by John Watkins, Church Information Form prepared by the 1980 Pastor Nominating Committee)

ABOUT THE AUTHOR

Melynda Dovel Wilcox is a freelance writer and editor, having previously worked for *Kiplinger's Personal Finance Magazine* for nearly 20 years. Her blog, *Port City Notebook* (portcitynotebook.com), covers education and other topics of interest to residents of Alexandria, Virginia, where she resides with her husband. Contact the author at melynda.wilcox@gmail.com.